JAMES K. POLK

1795 — 1849

Chronology—Documents—Bibliographical Aids

Edited by
JOHN J. FARRELL

Series Editor
HOWARD F. BREMER

1970
OCEANA PUBLICATIONS, INC.
Dobbs Ferry, New York

Printed in the United States of America

CONTENTS

EDITOR'S FOREWORD

Every attempt has been made to cite the most accurate dates in this Chronology. Diaries, documents, letters, and similar evidence have been used to determine the exact date. If, however, later scholarship has found such dates to be obviously erroneous, the more plausible date has been used. Should this Chronology be in conflict with other authorities, the student is urged to go back to original sources as well as to such careful biographers as Arthur Stanley Link.

This is a research tool compiled primarily for the student. While it does make some judgments on the significance of the events, it is hoped that they are reasoned judgments based on a long acquaintance with American History.

Obviously, the very selection of events by any writer is itself a judgment.

The essence of these little books is in their making available some pertinent facts and key documents *plus* a critical bibliography which should direct the student to investigate for himself additional and/or contradictory material. The works cited may not always be available in small libraries, but neither are they usually the old, out of print, type of book often included in similar accounts.

CHRONOLOGY

EARLY LIFE

1795

November 2 James Knox Polk, son of Samuel and Jane (Knox) Polk, born in Mecklenburg County, North Carolina. Eldest of ten children.

1806

Polk family settled in valley of Duck River, Tennessee.

1807

Maury County, Tennessee, organized at the instigation of the Polks.

1812

Had gallstones removed by Doctor Ephraim McDowell, a famous surgical pioneer, in Kentucky.

1813

July Enrolled as student in Zion Church Academy Day School near Columbia, Tennessee.

1815

Entered as student in Academy in Murfreesborough, Tennessee. Considered one of the most promising young men in school.

1816

January Entered sophomore class at University of North Carolina. Noted for his sense of duty and estimable behavior.

1817

Won prize winning essay on "American Liberty."

1818

May Graduated from University of North Carolina with first honors in mathematics and the classics. Returned to Tennessee, and practiced in law office of Felix Grundy.

1819

September 20 Elected clerk of Tennessee Senate; kept Senate journal, and was paid six dollars a day.

1820

Admitted to the bar, Maury County, Tennessee, and practiced law at Columbia. He developed a very successful practice within one year.

1821

Chosen captain of local militia, later a major in Columbia, Tennessee.

1823

September Entered Tennessee State legislature for two years; built friendship with Andrew Jackson. David Crockett also elected from Tennessee's western territory. Took a critical stand against banking interests, and spirited a drive for federal land grants for the establishment of schools.

1824

January 1 Married Sarah Childress of Murfreesborough, Tennessee. Sarah had stern religious principles against dancing and drinking. Her dedication to her husband's political success was noteworthy.

August 31 Ezekiel Polk, James' grandfather, died on frontier, western Tennessee, leaving thousands of acres of land and twenty-four slaves.

1825

Helped to honor General Lafayette on a visit to Nashville.

August Elected to United States House of Representatives, as a loyal proponent of Jacksonian thought. Polk defended Jackson when the hero of New Orleans was under investigation in Congress for killing six militiamen.

October Journeyed on horseback eastward over the mountains and the new National Road to Baltimore, then by train to Washington, D.C. to take his seat in Congress. The Capitol was nearing completion, and the heavy columns of the portico were being swung into place. There were still no stairs from the square to the main floor.

Proposed abolishing the Electoral College system for a system providing direct popular election of the President.

1827

August Relected by wide margin by Maury County voters for second term in House of Representatives.

October Returned to Washington for second term in office; appointed to Committee on Foreign Affairs. Took a firm stand against protective tariff, and advocated strict construction of the Constitution.

November Samuel Polk, James' father, died. James, as the eldest son, inherited responsibilities for distribution of property, and the care for the younger children.

1828

June-July Campaigned for the election of Andrew Jackson; rode horseback from one end of Tennessee to the other. After the election of Jackson, Polk arranged the triumphal trip for the new President from Nashville to Washington, D.C.

1829

As United States Congressman he supported Jackson in all his political trials, opposed nullification as an extreme measure, and consistently voted against federal funds for internal improvements.

1831

January Brother, Frank, died of acute alcoholism.

May Brother Marshall died; a third brother, John, died a few months later.

Strongly opposed Henry Clay's American System.

1832

July 10 Jackson vetoed bill for the rechartering of the National Bank.

October South Carolina legislature declared tariffs of 1828 and 1832 null and void.

November Whig Party emerged in opposition to Jackson's policies. Jackson reelected President.

December Polk, on House Ways and Means Committee, authored a Compromise tariff to placate South Carolina's objections; he later supported Henry Clay's famous compromise.

1833

August   Reelected United States Congressman from Maury County; ran as a loyal Jacksonian.

August   Inclined religiously to support the Methodist Episcopal Church, but did not become a member of the denomination.

October   Lost bid for Speaker of House to Congressman John Bell, a Whig and a fellow Tennessean, by lack of ten votes.

December   Made Chairman of House Ways and Means Committee, and had all questions related to the United States Bank's irresponsibility referred to the Committee.

December 30   Emerged as a nationally recognized figure after delivering a powerful speech concluding that the U.S. Bank's lack of self-discipline had made deposit removal necessary.

1834

June   Supported the distribution of United States hard specie to state banks, and acted as the indisputed voice of the Administration in most matters before Congress. Jackson considered him to be his finest spokesman.

August   Announced support of Martin Van Buren to succeed Jackson.

September   Sold plantation in western Tennessee, and bought new cotton land in north central Mississippi.

                  Enjoyed his first ride on the new rail line connecting Baltimore and Washington, D.C.

1835

August   Reelected United States Congressman from Maury County.

December 7   Chosen Speaker of the House. Defeated nearest rival, John Bell, 132-84. Deliberated and acted as a loyal Jacksonian. Was a constant target for the abusive Whigs and Nullifiers.

1836

May   Texas revolution concluded; question of slavery became an issue in the election of a new President.

November   Martin Van Buren elected President.

December   All questions relating to slavery were ignored under the provisions of the "gag" resolution, passed by the House. Polk supported the resolution, voting with the majority over the protesting John Quincy Adams.

1837

March   Polk accompanied Jackson home to Nashville from Washington. Enjoyed the tumultuous public demonstrations of affection accorded the former President.

May   Massive economic problems brought about a major depression. Elections in Tennessee returned only three Democratic congressmen to office, Polk among them.

October   Brother Samuel suspended from Yale University for participating in a riot; he moved to Washington to live with James and Sarah.

1838

August 30   Announced candidacy for governorship of Tennessee; spent next two months speaking to electorate throughout the state. Accused by the opposition of attempting to "Polk Van Burenism down the throats of our citizens."

November   Left for his last session as United States Congressman.

1839

April-   Rode 1300 miles on horseback throughout Tennessee cam-
June   paigning for the governorship.

August 9   Elected governor of Tennessee with a majority of 2,462 votes.

October 14   Inaugurated governor of Tennessee, in Nashville; ex-President Andrew Jackson in attendance. Inaugural Address stated the belief that final constitutional authority rested with the people of the Republic, and not the states, as proclaimed by Senator John C. Calhoun of South Carolina. Was first governor of Tennessee to function as a party leader.

June   Wrote to President Martin Van Buren, suggesting himself as a candidate for Vice-President in the coming national election.

1840

July 4　Announced candidacy for reelection as governor of Tennessee. Opposed by James C. Jones, Whig candidate, whose use of "coonery and foolery" made him a great favorite with the Tennessee people.

November　William Henry Harrison elected President of the United States. A defeat for the Democratic Party.

1841

April 4　President William Henry Harrison died in office; John Tyler, Vice-Presidency, assumed the Presidency.

August　Lost governorship of Tennessee to James C. ("Slim Jim") Jones.

November　Left Nashville and returned home to Columbia, Tennessee.

1842

May 7　Ex-President Martin Van Buren visited with Polk at his residence in Columbia.

June-
July　Traveled to Philadelphia and New York to win political support for nomination for Democratic Vice-Presidency in the next election.

1843

August　Defeated again for governorship of Tennessee by incumbent James C. Jones. Called defeat the "darkest hour of my political life."

December　Representative from the Texas Republic openly pleaded for immediate annexation to the United States in a speech before the House of Representatives.

1844

April　Actively sought nomination as Democratic Vice-Presidential candidate.

Democratic party bitterly divided on the issue of national candidates. Martin Van Buren of New York, John C. Calhoun of South Carolina, Lewis Cass of Michigan, and James Buchanan of Pennsylvania were considered most favored sons for the position of Chief Executive. Each man's stand on the slavery question would be the major factor in his selection.

April 12 President John Tyler announced annexation treaty with Texas. Senate would have to confirm the treaty. This action made annexation a dominant political issue.

April 21 Wrote his "Texas letter," which was reprinted in all reputable journals in the country. Declared himself for "immediate reannexation" of Texas. Also included the Oregon country as rightfully belonging to the American people. Letter had the effect of having Polk seriously considered as a possible candidate for President or Vice-President.

May 1 Whig party Convention, Baltimore, Maryland. Henry Clay of Kentucky was nominated on the first ballot. Theodore Frelinghuysen of New Jersey was nominated as the Vice-Presidential candidate.

May 10 Ex-President Jackson, at The Hermitage, summoned caucus to discuss Texas; he declared Martin Van Buren had committed "suicide" and could not be elected. Jackson suggested Polk as a logical nominee.

May 27-30 Democratic convention in Baltimore, Maryland. Rule requiring two-thirds vote to win nomination for Presidency caused consternation. The total number of votes was 266. The number required for selection was 177. Polk was not nominated on the first seven ballots.

The candidates on the first ballot, and the votes they received were:
>Martin Van Buren, New York, 146
>Lewis Cass, Michigan, 83
>Cave Johnson, Tennessee, 24
>John C. Calhoun, South Carolina, 6
>James Buchanan, Pennsylvania, 4
>Levi Woodbury, New Hampshire, 2
>John Stewart, Connecticut, 1

In case of stalemate, the plan, originally, was to nominate Silas Wright of New York as a compromise candidate. Polk would become Wright's Vice-Presidential candidate. Wright would not accept the nomination for the Presidency, and Polk became the compromise candidate.

Polk nominated for Presidency on eighth ballot by George Bancroft (historian and delegate from Massachusetts.) Bancroft suggested Polk as a compromise candidate to break stalemate between Martin Van Buren of New York, and Lewis Cass of Michigan. Polk received 44 votes, Van Buren 104, and Cass 114 on the eighth ballot.

Polk elected unanimously on ninth ballot (May 29).

First "dark-horse" candidate for the Presidency, and first Presidential candidate to be chosen because of a deadlock.

News of Polk's selection was carried from Baltimore to Washington, D.C. over the newly strung telegraph.

Democratic party's platform included the following planks: (1) All the lands included in the Oregon territory rightfully belonged to the United States, (2) No part of the Oregon country should be ceded to the United States, (3) Reoccupation of Oregon and reannexation of Texas should be short-ranged goals for the nation.

Silas Wright of New York was chosen Vice-Presidential candidate, but he declined the nomination. George Mifflin Dallas of Pennsylvania accepted the position as Polk's running mate. A former Senator from Pennsylvania (1831-1833), Dallas represented a moderate northern point of view, and balanced the ticket. The nomination of Dallas gave the Democrats their slogan "Polk and Dallas—Texas and Oregon."

The Democratic party's campaign slogan "Fifty-four forty or Fight," referring to the northern limits of the Oregon country, was used to draw northern and western expansionist votes. The slogan's creation has been attributed to Senator William Allen of Ohio or to Samuel Medary, of the *Ohio Statesman*.

Whig fury at his nomination gave rise to unwarranted and exaggerated jibe, "Who is James K. Polk?"

June 11　　　Received official announcement of his nomination. Declared in his letter of acceptance a settled purpose of being a candidate for reelection, if elected.

August　　　Dubbed "Young Hickory" in New York City press.

November 14 Elected President of the United States. Received 170 Electoral votes to Henry Clay's 105; led popular vote by 1.4% over Clay, the closest Presidential election at that time in terms of popular vote.

The final popular vote: Polk, 1,337,243; Clay, 1,299,068; Birney, 62,000.

James Gillespie Birney, New York, candidate for the Liberty Party, received enough popular votes in New York State to keep Henry Clay from winning the electoral votes of that state. If Clay had taken New York's electoral vote, he would have been President.

Ex-President Andrew Jackson, upon hearing the news of Polk's election, thanked God that He had permitted him to live long enough to see the country in safe hands.

Last Presidential election to be held under the State preference system for selecting the day for Presidential voting. Under this system each state could choose its own day, but the elections had to be held thirty-four days before the first Wednesday in December, the date for the Presidential electors to meet. A federal act was passed on January 23, 1845, requiring the Presidential election to be held on the first Tuesday after the first Monday in November.

December 3 Gag rule, against presentation of anti-slavery petitions in the House of Representatives, repealed.

1845

February 13 Arrived in Washington, D.C. after trip from Columbia, Tennessee, via horseback, steamboat, and rail.

March 1 President John Tyler signed joint congressional resolution for the annexation of Texas.

TERM IN OFFICE

March 4 Inaugurated as eleventh President of the United States, and, at fifty years of age, the youngest President at that time. Chief Justice Roger B. Taney administered the oath of office. Polk presented a detailed plan for his administration in his inaugural address, including United States rights to the Oregon country as "clear and unquestionable." He lauded the idea of Union, and mentioned his aversion to sectional strife. *(See* Documents.)

March 6   James Buchanan, Pennsylvania, appointed Secretary of State, replacing John C. Calhoun, South Carolina. Calhoun was not fond of Polk.

Robert James Walker, Mississippi, appointed Secretary of Treasury, replacing George Mortimer Bibb, Kentucky, from previous administration.

William Learned Marcy, New York, appointed Secretary of War, replacing William Wilkins, Pennsylvania, from previous administration. Marcy was an important political appointment from a state that had narrowly favored Polk for the Presidency.

John Young Mason, Virginia, appointed Attorney General, replacing John Nelson, Maryland, from previous administration.

Cave Johnson, Tennessee, appointed Postmaster General, replacing Charles Anderson Wickliffe, Kentucky, from previous administration. Cave Johnson was one of Polk's very few close friends.

March 10   George Bancroft, Massachusetts, appointed Secretary of Navy, replacing John Young Mason, from previous administration. John Young Mason had received appointment as Polk's Attorney General.

March 28   Mexico broke diplomatic relations with the United States. Mexico interpreted the United States annexation of Texas as "an act of aggression." Specific disagreements were: (1) the disputed boundary line of the southwestern part of Texas. Mexico insisted that the line was along the Nueces River. Texas claimed the line to be along the Rio Grande River, which, Texas insisted, was part of the Mexican-Texas Treaty of 1836. The United States government upheld the claims of Texas as legitimate, having been based on the Adams-Onis Treaty of 1819. (2) The refusal of Mexico to pay more than two million dollars owed to United States citizens who held claims against Mexico. (3) The dispute concerning California. The United States resented Mexico's orders to remove American settlers from California, and questioned Mexico's friendly relations with British agents, who were suspected to be involved in forming plans for an eventual seizure of California.

March 29   Sent William S. Parrott to Mexico City to deal in "a liberal and friendly spirit" with Mexican authorities.

June 8   Ex-President Andrew Jackson died at The Hermitage.

June 15   Ordered General Zachary Taylor's army to "some point on or near the Rio Grande River."

June 16   Congress of Texas Republic voted unanimously for "reentry" into the United States.

June 24   Secretary of Navy Bancroft ordered, in the event of war with Mexico, to seize and occupy California ports.

June   Revealed to Secretary Bancroft that there were four measures which were to be the goals of his administration. These were: a reduction of the tariff, an independent Treasury, the settlement of the Oregon boundary, and the acquisition of California.

July 31   General Zachary Taylor moved his forces to the south bank of the Nueces River.

August 6   Ordered immediate reinforcement to Taylor's army in Texas.

August 26   Ordered General Taylor to regard any attempt by Mexican forces to cross the Rio Grande as "the commencement of hostilities."

September 16   Appointed John Slidell as United States envoy extraordinary and minister plenipotentiary to Mexico. Mexico had not agreed to reopen diplomatic relations with the United States. John Slidell was to act secretly for the purchase of Upper California and New Mexico, and for a settlement of the southwestern boundary of Texas. Mexico had agreed, beforehand, to discuss only the Texas boundary, and only with a non-diplomatic agent.

September 20   Appointed Levi Woodbury of New Hampshire, former Senator and Secretary of Treasury, as Associate Justice to the Supreme Court, replacing Associate Justice Robert Baldwin of Connecticut, who had resigned.

October 10   Secretary of Navy George Bancroft officially opened the "Naval School," Annapolis, Maryland. Later called the United States Naval Academy.

October 15   Mexico agreed to receive a "commissioner" from the United States, but refused to negotiate with a United States envoy extraordinary and minister plenipotentiary, as was John Slidell.

October 17   Commodore Robert F. Stockton given sealed orders to proceed to Monterey, California, and to aid Commodore John D. Sloat in seizing sections of California in the event of war with Mexico.

November 7   Decided to send John Slidell, immediately, as an envoy extraordinary and minister plenipotentiary to negotiate with Mexican government. This was done with the full knowledge that such a representative would not be acceptable by the Mexican government.

November 10   John Slidell presented American demands to Mexican government.

December   "Manifest Destiny" phrase begun to be used by popular press. The phrase apparently employed for the first time in an expansionist journal, *The United States Magazine and Democratic Review*. John L. O'Sullivan, the editor of the journal, was given credit for its inception. The idea of Divine Providence bequeathing the right of expansion to the people of the United States was popularly accepted.

December 2   First Annual Message presented to Congress. (*See* Documents).

December 16   John Slidell told by the Mexican government that he was not acceptable as a negotiator, and that Mexico would discuss nothing except the possible solution to the Texas boundary.

December 27   British Minister to the United States, Richard Pakenham, reversing himself, asked that the 49th parallel as a solution to United States-British dispute of the Oregon boundary, be submitted for arbitration. President Polk would not do so. Not wanting to appear as a weak man, Polk preferred to "hold the line" against the British.

The cry "Fifty-four forty or fight," describing the northern limit of the United States claim to the Oregon country, had become a symbol for a strong, determined America against the intrigues of Great Britain. Polk's party support in Congress depended on the expansionists, who subscribed to a strong stand against Great Britain.

December 28   Signed bill admitting Texas to the Union.

December 31   Mexican President Jose J. Herrera overthrown by General Mariano Paredes.

1846

January 4   President Mariano Paredes became Mexico's new leader. Paredes stated that he would defend Mexico's territory against the United States.

January 12   Great Britain again announced willingness to compromise on the Oregon claims.

January 13   Ordered General Taylor's forces to march to north bank of the Rio Grande, after receiving letter from John Slidell citing Mexico's refusal to negotiate.

February 26   Secretary of State Buchanan informed Louis McLane, United States minister in London, to be receptive to British overtures to reopen discussions relating to the Oregon territory.

February 4   Restated opposition to an arbitrated settlement with Great Britain with relation to the Oregon Country.

March 8   General Zachary Taylor began advancing his forces to the Rio Grande.

April 12   General Zachary Taylor warned by Mexican commander to withdraw back to Nueces River. Taylor refused to consider a withdrawal.

April 27   Signed a joint Congressional resolution terminating United States-Great Britain joint occupation of the Oregon country.

April 28   Learned that John Slidell had been refused recognition as an American diplomatic minister by the Mexican government. Slidell expressed his contempt for the Mexican people in a personal letter to Secretary Buchanan. Polk instructed Buchanan to begin drafting a war message.

May 8   Heard that a Mexican force had crossed the Rio Grande, and had killed or wounded sixteen United States cavalrymen.

                Battle of Palo Alto, on the road to Matamores. United States forces compelled Mexican cavalry to retreat.

May 9   Battle of Resaca de la Palma. Mexican army fled across the Rio Grande, pursued by American forces.

May 11   Drafted a war message, and delivered it to Congress. Stated that Mexican attitudes of "belligerence and unreasonableness" caused the conflict. Asked Congress to "recognize the existence of war." Polk avered that Mexico had shed American blood on American soil.

May 13   Congress declared that a state of war existed with Mexico.

May 30   Ordered Colonel Stephen Watts Kearney to proceed with United States cavalry to California from Fort Leavenworth. Kearney was to seize as much Mexican territory as possible enroute to California.

June 12   Sent British compromise proposals, relating to the Oregon dispute, to the Senate. Polk did not want to appear vacillating on his previous stand, and asked the Senate for its advice.

June 14   Bear Flag Republic created by American revolutionists in Sonoma, California.

June 15   Senate advised Polk to accept British compromise proposals for the settlement of the Oregon controversy. Proposals for the compromise were included in a treaty and ratified, 41-14. The provisions of the Oregon Treaty included the acceptance of the 49th parallel as the boundary between the United States and Canada, and rights of free navigation for both countries. (*See* Documents.)

June 19   Monterey, California, fell to the forces of Captain John Fremont.

June 6   Lord Aberdeen, British Foreign Secretary, submitted Great Britain's proposals for compromise talks related to the Oregon controversy.

July 9   Forces of Commander John B. Montgomery seized San Francisco, while Lieutenant James W. Revere took Sonoma. The American flag replaced the Bear Flag.

July 12   Ordered Commodore John D. Sloat's naval forces to seize San Diego, California.

July 30   Walker Tariff passed. Provided for a downward revision of tariff rates, and reversed the trend towards high rates. Although still protectionist the Walker tariff greatly reduced duties, and set pace for further reductions in later years.

August 3   Vetoed a bill providing for Federal funds for internal improvements.

August 5   Appointed Robert C. Grier of Pennsylvania Associate Justice to the Supreme Court. Grier replaced the late Associate Justice Joseph Story of Massachusetts.

August 8   Congressman David Wilmot of Pennsylvania, formerly a Polk supporter, introduced his famous proviso as an amendment to a war appropriations measure prohibiting slavery in all lands won from Mexico. Proviso was passed, narrowly, in the House, but defeated in the Senate.

Signed bill authorizing the reestablishment of the Independent Treasury System. (*See* Documents.)

August 13   Major Robert F. Stockton's forces occupied Santa Barbara and Los Angeles, California.

August 17   Major Robert F. Stockton announced the annexation of California by the United States.

Colonel Stephen Watts Kearney, having occupied Las Vegas, declared New Mexico part of the United States.

August 18   Forces of Colonel Kearney occupied Santa Fe.

September 9   Secretary of Navy Bancroft appointed United States minister to Great Britain. Replaced by John Young Mason of Virginia.

September 25   General William J. Worth, having secured control of western sectors, and after a four day seige, forced the surrender of Mexican forces at Monterey. General Zachary Taylor, after the battle, called an eight-week armistice. Polk did not approve, and questioned the possible political motives of General Taylor.

September 30   Mexicans in California successfully revolted against the United States occupation forces. Los Angeles, Santa Barbara, and San Diego were retaken by Mexican forces.

November   Results of State and Congressional elections showed gains for Whig party. The Whigs capitalized on anti-war feelings, and on Polk's opposition to internal improvements and high tariff. A small majority gave the Whigs control of the House of Representatives.

1847

January 10   Combined naval and land forces of Colonel Stephen Kearny and Major Robert Stockton reestablished American presence in Los Angeles.

January 13   General Andres Pico, leader of Mexican forces in the San Fernando Valley, surrendered the last of any effective fighting forces in California to Captain John Fremont.

February 23   General Zachary Taylor's army won the difficult and important battle at Buena Vista. General Santa Anna's forces retired from the northern provinces of Mexico.

March 21   General Santa Anna took oath as President of Mexico.

March 29   General Winfield S. Scott, with 10,000 men and an invasion fleet, formally occupied Vera Cruz. This was the first large amphibious action in United States history.

April 10	Sent Nicholas P. Trist with General Scott's army to arrange for a peace settlement with Mexico. Trist was the chief clerk of the State Department. Although assigned on a "confidential mission" by Polk, almost all of official Washington was aware of Trist's assignment within three days.
April 18	An assault by United States forces on the army of General Santa Anna gave the American army control of Cerro Gordo, an important position on route to Mexico City.
May 1	Laid cornerstone of building to be called the Smithsonian Insitute.
May 17	Mentioned publicly the heroic behavior of Colonel Jefferson Davis, wounded at Buena Vista.
May 20	Posed for portrait done by Thomas Sully.
June 7	Met with Kit Carson, in Washington, to discuss events in California.
June 22- July 7	Toured the North—Philadelphia, New York, and parts of New England. Received cordially in all states.
September 4	From his diary, "With me it is emphatically true that the Presidency is 'no bed of roses.'"
September 6	Negotiations for peace, between Nicholas Trist and former Mexican President Herrera, came to an end. Mexico could not accept the conditions for peace presented by Trist.
September 8	United States forces successfully took Mexican fortifications at the Battle of Molino del Rey, outside the gates of Mexico City.
September 13	Chapultepec Hill and the Mexican Military College on the crest of the hill were taken by United States forces. "Los Ninos," about one hundred Mexican boys from the Military College, defended the hill until the end.
September 14	Mexico City fell to United States forces. The American flag was flown over the Mexican National Palace.

October 4   Recalled Trist as confidential commissioner to Mexico. Felt that too much time had been wasted by the negotiator.

October 20   Learned that General Scott's forces had taken Mexico City.

November 2   Fifty-second birthday. Looked forward to retiring to private life.

December 23 Told Secretary of State James Buchanan he would not produce a "favorite son" candidate at the coming Democratic Convention. Polk kept an absolutely neutral position on this issue. Nothing in his diary indicates any preference for eventual leadership of the Democratic party.

1848

January 15   Received dispatches from Nicholas Trist announcing that negotiations were proceeding with Mexico in spite of Trist's having been recalled.

January 28   Gold discovered on the property of Johann Augustus Sutter in lower Sacramento Valley, on a branch of the American River.

February 2   Treaty of Guadalupe-Hidalgo completed and signed by Commissioner Nicholas Trist and acting Mexican President Pena y Pena. Trist refused to cease negotiations after reception of his letter from Polk asking him to return to the United States.

February 18 Received news that Trist had arrived in the United States with a treaty already agreed to by the Mexican Government. Polk accepted the treaty, but Trist was severely criticized by the President.

March 10   Senate ratified Trist's treaty of Guadalupe-Hidalgo. (*See* Documents.)

Mentioned, privately, he would like to see Cuba part of the United States.

May 22   Democratic National Convention, Baltimore, Maryland, nominated General Lewis Cass of Michigan as its candidate for President. General William O. Butler of Kentucky was chosen Vice-Presidential candidate. General Cass believed in "popular sovereignty" as a solution to the slavery expansion problem. The Democratic platform stated that Congress should play no role in deciding on status of slavery in the states, and should not interfere with slavery in the territories.

Polk, true to his word, would not favor any candidate at the Convention. He agreed to support the choice of the Democratic party. Polk, privately, was not enthusiastic about General Cass.

May 25   Mexican Congress ratified Treaty of Guadalupe-Hidalgo.

June 7   General Zachary Taylor chosen Presidential candidate by the Whig party at Philadelphia Convention. Millard Fillmore of New York chosen as the Vice-Presidential candidate. The choice of General Taylor revolved around his competence as a military man.

June 12   American forces withdrew from Mexico City.

June 21   Isaac Toucey of Connecticut appointed Attorney General. Replaced Nathan Clifford of Maine, who was sent to Mexico to assist in final ratification of the peace treaty.

June 22   The factional Democrats, called Barnburners because of their efforts to "burn the Democratic barn," met in Convention at Utica, New York. Ex-President Martin Van Buren of New York and Henry Dodge of Wisconsin were its chosen candidates for President and Vice-President. Van Buren, affronted by political slights of the Polk administration, attempted to regain control of the Democratic party.

June 24   Urged that the Missouri Compromise line be drawn through the new United States territories.

July 4   Proclaimed the Treaty of Guadalupe-Hidalgo in effect.

               Laid cornerstone of the Washington Monument.

July 19   Women's Convention at Seneca Falls, New York, adopted a series of resolutions proclaiming equal rights for women. Convention under the leadership of Lucretia Mott and Elizabeth Cady Stanton.

August 2   The remaining United States forces in Mexico left Vera
                   Cruz.

August 9   Free-Soil party met at Buffalo, New York, to choose a
                   Presidential candidate who would represent the opposition
                   on the question of slavery expansion. Various dissatisfied
                   factions united on the principles enumerated in the Wilmot
                   Proviso. Martin Van Buren was chosen as the Presidential
                   candidate and Charles Francis Adams of Massachusetts
                   as his running-mate. The slogan of the Free-Soilers was,
                   "Free soil, free speech, free labor, and free men."

August 14   Signed bill authorizing the admittance of Oregon as a
                   territory of the United States. The bill specifically forbade
                   slavery in the new territory. The question of slavery in the
                   new territories was increasingly debated during this time.

September 10   Attended service at First Presbyterian Church in Washington
                   to hear the Reverend Dr. William McGuffey (compiler of
                   the famous series of readers) preach. Polk was much
                   impressed.

September   John Frémont set up an "independent government" in
                   California. Polk annoyed with independent attitude of
                   Fremont.

November 2   Turned fifty-three years of age; philosophized on the futility
                   of worldly honors.

November 7   General Zachary Taylor, Whig candidate, elected President
                   of the United States. First occasion in United States history
                   when all states voted on the same day. Polk felt election of
                   Taylor was regrettable.

                   Enough support was probably drained from the regular
                   Democratic party by the Free-Soilers to enable General
                   Taylor to take New York's 36 electoral votes.

December 7   Received specimens of gold from California. His personal
                   excitement, and his public pronouncements concerning the
                   discovery of gold had a great deal to do with the rush to
                   California in 1849. (*See* Fourth Annual Message in
                   Documents.)

December 13   House of Representatives approved the Wilmot Proviso.

December 23   Felt that agitation against slave trade in Washington, D.C. was "mischievous and wicked."

1849

January 16   Criticized Senator John C. Calhoun's intransigent attitude related to the question of slavery. Told Calhoun personally that the Senator's extremism on the subject would hurt the nation. Polk upheld the right of popular sovereignty in the western territories.

January 30   Told Cabinet that he would veto any bill that would authorize use of federal funds to construct a road across the Isthmus of Panama.

February 7   Entertained at White House, with "venerable Mrs. Madison" on his arm.

February 13   Remarked that his four years as President were "Four years of incessant labor and anxiety, and of great responsibility."

February 14   Posed for Matthew C. Brady for daguerreotype likeness.

March 1   Entertained President-elect Taylor at White House dinner.

March 3   Last working day as President. Spent hours at Capitol in order to instantly veto pending legislation that would include aspects of Wilmot Proviso.

Congress created Department of Interior.

March 5   Accompanied General Taylor in open carriage to Presidential inauguration. Noted in diary that Taylor was "a well-meaning old man. He is, however, uneducated, exceedingly ignorant of public affairs, and, I should judge, of very ordinary capacity."

Left that evening for Tennessee.

RETIREMENT

March 6-   Triumphal tour of Southern cities on return to Nashville.
April 2   Became extremely ill in cholera atmosphere. Arrived in Nashville exhausted and in critical condition.

June 15   Died in Nashville at age fifty-three, after four months in retirement. Was baptized by a Methodist minister six days before his death. Buried in his garden at Nashville.

Sarah Childress Polk lived for forty-two years after the death of her husband. She remained in her residence at Nashville, and during the Civil War kept strictly neutral in her position. Orders were given to the Union forces not to disturb Mrs. Polk or any of her household.

In 1893, the remains of Polk, and those of his wife, were reinterred on the state capital grounds in Nashville.

DOCUMENTS

INAUGURAL ADDRESS
March 4, 1845

In 1845, James K. Polk was inaugurated as the youngest President in American history. His Address was definitive in setting his Presidential objectives. In the Address, the President made the following points, thus charting the direction the country was to take for the next four years: (1) The concept of Union was exalted; (2) Sectionalism was considered dangerous to the nation; (3) Tariff was more than a "protective device"; (4) the United States title to the Oregon country was "clear and unquestionable."

Fellow-Citizens:

Without solicitation on my part, I have been chosen by the free and voluntary suffrages of my countrymen to the most honorable and most responsible office on earth. I am deeply impressed with gratitude for the confidence reposed in me. Honored with this distinguished consideration at an earlier period of life than any of my predecessors, I can not disguise the diffidence with which I am about to enter on the discharge of my official duties.

If the more aged and experienced men who have filled the office of President of the United States even in the infancy of the Republic distrusted their ability to discharge the duties of that exalted station, what ought not to be the apprehensions of one so much younger and less endowed now that our domain extends from ocean to ocean, that our people have so greatly increased in numbers, and at a time when so great diversity of opinion prevails in regard to the principles and policy which should characterize the administration of our Government? Well may the boldest fear and the wisest tremble when incurring responsibilities on which may depend our country's peace and prosperity, and in some degree the hopes and happiness of the whole human family.

In assuming responsibilities so vast I fervently invoke the aid of that Almighty Ruler of the Universe in whose hands are the destinies of nations and of men to guard this Heaven-favored land against the mischiefs which without His guidance might arise from an unwise public policy. With a firm

‡*James Richardson, ed. *Messages and Papers of The Presidents,* Vol. 5, New York, 1897, pp. 2223-2232.

reliance upon the wisdom of Omnipotence to sustain and direct me in the path of duty which I am appointed to pursue, I stand in the presence of this assembled multitude of my countrymen to take upon myself the solemn obligation "to the best of my ability to preserve, protect, and defend the Constitution of the United States."

A concise enumeration of the principles which will guide me in the administrative policy of the Government is not only in accordance with the examples set me by all my predecessors, but is eminently befitting the occasion.

The Constitution itself, plainly written as it is, the safeguard for our federative compact, the offspring of concession and compromise, binding together in the bonds of peace and union this great and increasing family of free and independent States, will be the chart by which I shall be directed.

It will be my first care to administer the Government in the true spirit of that instrument, and to assume no powers not expressly granted or clearly implied in its terms. The Government of the United States is one of delegated and limited powers, and it is by a strict adherence to the clearly granted powers and by abstaining from the exercise of doubtful or unauthorized implied powers that we have the only sure guaranty against the recurrence of those unfortunate collisions between the Federal and State authorities which have occasionally so much disturbed the harmony of our system and even threatened the perpetuity of our glorious Union.

"To the States, respectively, or to the people" have been reserved "the powers not delegated to the United States by the Constitution nor prohibited by it to the States." Each State is a complete sovereignty within the sphere of its reserved powers. The Government of the Union, acting within the sphere of its delegated authority not clearly delegated to it, the States should be equally careful that in the maintenance of their rights they do not overstep the limits of powers reserved to them. One of the most distinguished of my predecessors attached deserved importance to "the support of the State governments in all their rights, as the most competent administration for our domestic concerns and the surest bulwark against antirepublican tendencies," and to the "preservation of the General Government in its whole constitutional vigor, as the sheet anchor of our peace at home and safety abroad."

To the Government of the United States has been intrusted the exclusive management of our foreign affairs. Beyond that it wields a few general enumerated powers. It does not force reform on the States. It leaves individuals, over whom it casts its protecting influence, entirely free to improve their own condition by the legitimate exercise of all their mental and physical powers. It is a common protector of each and all the States; of every man who lives upon our soil, whether of native or foreign birth; of every religious sect, in their worship of the Almighty according to the dictates of their own conscience; of every shade of opinion, and the most free inquiry; of every art, trade, and occupation consistent with the laws of the States. And we rejoice in the general happiness, prosperity, and advancement of our country, which have been the offspring of freedom, and not of power.

This most admirable and wisest system of well-regulated self-government among men ever devised by human minds has been tested by its successful operation for more than half a century, and if preserved from the usurpations of the Federal Government on the one hand and the exercise by the States of powers not reserved to them on the other, will, I fervently hope and believe, endure for ages to come and dispense the blessings of civil and religious liberty to distant generations. To effect objects so dear to every patriot I shall devote myself with anxious solicitude. It will be my desire to guard against that most fruitful source of danger to the harmonious action of our system which consists in substituting the mere discretion and caprice of the Executive or of majorities in the legislative department of the Government for powers which have been withheld from the Federal Government by the Constitution. By the theory of our Government majorities rule, but this right is not an arbitrary or unlimited one. It is a right to be exercised in subordination to the Constitution and in conformity to it. One great object of the Constitution was to restrain majorities from oppressing minorities or encroaching upon their just rights. Minorities have a right to appeal to the Constitution as a shield against such oppression.

That the blessings of liberty which our Constitution secures may be enjoyed alike by minorities and majorities, the Executive has been wisely invested with a qualified veto upon the acts of the Legislature. It is a negative power, and is conservative in its character. It arrests for the time hasty, inconsiderate, or unconstitutional legislation, invites reconsideration, and transfers questions at issue between the legislative and executive departments to the tribunal of the people. Like all other powers, it is subject to be abused. When judiciously and properly exercised, the Constitution itself may be saved from infraction and the rights of all preserved and protected.

The inestimable value of our Federal Union is felt and acknowledged by all. By this system of united and confederated States our people are permitted collectively and individually to seek their own happiness in their own way, and the consequences have been most auspicious. Since the Union was formed the number of the States has increased from thirteen to twenty-eight; two of these have taken their position as members of the Confederacy within the last week. Our population has increased from three to twenty millions. New communities and States are seeking protection under its aegis, and multitudes from the Old World are flocking to our shores to participate in its blessings. Beneath its benign sway peace and prosperity prevail. Freed from the burdens and miseries of war, our trade and intercourse have extended throughout the world. Mind, no longer tasked in devising means to accomplish or resist schemes of ambition, usurpation, or conquest, is devoting itself to man's true interests in developing his faculties and powers and the capacity of nature to minister to his enjoyments. Genius is free to announce its inventions and discoveries, and the hand is free to accomplish whatever the head conceives not incompatible with the rights of a fellow-being. All distinctions of birth or of rank have been abolished. All citizens, whether native or adopted, are placed upon terms of precise equality. All are entitled to equal rights and equal protection. No union exists between church and state, and perfect freedom of opinion is guaranteed to all sects and creeds.

These are some of the blessings secured to our happy land by our Federal Union. To perpetuate them it is our sacred duty to preserve it. Who shall assign limits to the achievements of free minds and free hands under the protection of this glorious Union? No treason to mankind since the organization of society would be equal in atrocity to that of him who would lift his hand to destroy it. He would overthrow the noblest structure of human wisdom, which protects himself and his fellow-man. He would stop the progress of free government and involve his country either in anarchy or despotism. He would extinguish the fire of liberty, which warms and animates the hearts of happy millions and invites all the nations of the earth to imitate our example. If he say that error and wrong are committed in the administration of the Government, let him remember that nothing human can be perfect, and that under no other system of government revealed by Heaven or devised by man has reason been allowed so free and broad a scope to combat error. Has the sword of despots proved to be a safer or surer instrument of reform in government than enlightened reason? Does he expect to find among the ruins of this Union a happier abode for our swarming millions than they now have under it? Every lover of this country must shudder at the thought of the possibility of its dissolution, and will be ready to adopt the patriotic sentiment, "Our Federal Union—it must be preserved." To preserve it the compromises which alone enabled our father to form a common constitution for the government and protection of so many States and distinct communities, of such diversified habits, interests, and domestic institutions, must be sacredly and religiously observed. Any attempt to disturb or destroy these compromises, being terms of the compact of union, can lead to none other than the most ruinous and disastrous consequences.

It is a source of deep regret that in some sections of our country misguided persons have occasionally indulged in schemes and agitations whose object is the destruction of domestic institutions existing in other sections—institutions which existed at the adoption of the Constitution and were recognized and protected by it. All must see that if it were possoble for them to be successful in attaining their object the dissolution of the Union and the consequent destruction of our happy form of government must speedily follow.

I am happy to believe that at every period of our existence as a nation there has existed, and continues to exist, among the great mass of our people a devotion to the Union of the States which will shield and protect it against the moral treason of any who would seriously contemplate its destruction. To secure a continuance of that devotion the compromises of the Constitution must not only be preserved, but sectional jealousies and heartburnings must be discountenanced, and all should remember that they are members of the same political family, having a common destiny. To increase the attachment of our people to the Union, our laws should be just. Any policy which shall tend to favor monopolies or the peculiar interests of sections or classes must operate to the prejudice of the interest of their fellow-citizens, and should be avoided. If the compromises of the Constitution be preserved, if sectional jealousies and heartburnings be discountenanced, if our laws be just and the Government be practically administered strictly within the limits of power prescribed to it, we may discard all apprehensions for the safety of the Union.

With these views of the nature, character, and objects of the Government and the value of the Union, I shall steadily oppose the creation of those institutions and systems which in their nature tend to pervert it from its legitimate purposes and make it the instrument of sections, classes, and individuals. We need no national banks or other extraneous institutions planted around the Government to control or strengthen it in opposition to the will of its authors. Experience has taught us how unnecessary they are as auxiliaries of the public authorities—how impotent for good and how powerful for mischief.

Ours was intended to be plain and frugal government, and I shall regard it to be my duty to recommend to Congress and, as far as the Executive is concerned, to enforce by all the means within my power the strictest economy in the expenditure of the public money which may be compatible with the public interests.

A national debt has become almost an institution of European monarchies. It is viewed in some of them as an essential prop to existing governments. Melancholy is the condition of that people whose government can be sustained only by a system which periodically transfers large amounts from the labor of the many to the coffers of the few. Such a system is incompatible with the ends for which our republican Government was instituted. Under a wise policy the debts contracted in our Revolution and during the War of 1812 have been happily extinguished. By a judicious application of the revenues not required for other necessary purposes, it is not doubted

that the debt which has grown out of the circumstances of the last few years
may be speedily paid off.

I congratulate my fellow-citizens on the entire restoration of the credit
of the General Government of the Union and that of many of the States.
Happy would it be for the indebted States if they were freed from their liabilities, many of which were incautiously contracted. Although the Government of the Union is neither in a legal nor a moral sense bound for the
debts of the States, and it would be a violation of our compact of union to
assume them, yet we can not but feel a deep interest in seeing all the States
meet their public liabilities and pay off their just debts at the earliest practicable period. That they will do so as soon as it can be done without imposing
too heavy burdens on their citizens there is no reason to doubt. The sound
moral and honorable feeling of the people of the indebted States can not be
questioned, and we are happy to perceive a settled disposition on their part,
as their ability returns after a season of unexampled pecuniary embarrass-
ment, to pay off all just demands and to acquiesce in any reasonable measures
to accomplish that object.

One of the difficulties which we have had to encounter in the practical
administration of the Government consists in the adjustment of our revenue
laws and the levy of the taxes necessary for the support of Government. In
the general proposition that no money shall be collected than the necessities
of an economical administration shall require all parties seem to acquiesce.
Nor does there seem to be any material difference of opinion as to the absence
of right in the Government to tax one section of country, or one class of
citizens, or one occupation, for the mere profit of another. "Justice and
sound policy forbid the Federal Government to foster one branch of industry to the detriment of another, or to cherish the interests of one portion
to the injury of another portion of our common country." I have heretofore
declared to my fellow-citizens that "in my judgment it is the duty of the
Government to extend, as far as it may be practicable to do so, by its
revenue laws and all other means within its power, fair and just protection
to all of the great interests of the whole Union, embracing agriculture,
manufacturers, the mechanic arts, commerce, and navigation." I have also
declared my opinion to be "in favor of a tariff for revenue," and that "in
adjusting the details of such a tariff I have sanctioned such moderate
discriminating duties as would produce the amount of revenue needed and at
the same time afford reasonable incidental protection to our home industry," and that I was "opposed to a tariff for protection merely, and not
for revenue."

The power "to lay and collect taxes, duties, imposts, and excises" was an
indispensable one to be conferred on the Federal Government, which without it would possess no means of providing for its own support. In execut-
ing this power by levying a tariff of duties for the support of Government,

the raising of *revenue* should be the *object* and *protection* the *incident*. To reverse this principle and make *protection* the *object* and *revenue* the *incident* would be to inflict manifest injustice upon all other than the protected interests. In levying duties for revenue it is doubtless proper to make such discriminations within the *revenue principle* as will afford incidental protection to our home interests. Within the revenue limit there is a discretion to discriminate; beyond that limit the rightful exercise of the power is not conceded. The incidental protection afforded to our home interests by discriminations within the revenue range it is believed will be ample. In making discriminations all our home interests should as far as practicable be equally protected. The largest protion of our people are agriculturists. Others are employed in manufactures, commerce, navigation, and the mechanic arts. They are all engaged in their respective pursuits and their joint labors constitute the national or home industry. To tax one branch of this home industry for the benefit of another would be unjust. No one of these interests can rightfully claim an advantage over the others, or to be enriched by impoverishing the others. All are equally entitled to the fostering care and protection of the Government. In exercising a sound discretion in levying discriminating duties within the limit prescribed, care should be taken that it be done in a manner not to benefit the wealthy few at the expense of the toiling millions by taxing *lowest* the luxuries of life, or articles of superior quality and high price, which can only be consumed by the wealthy, and *highest* the necessaries of life, or articles of coarse quality and low price, which the poor and great mass of our people must consume. The burdens of government should as far as practicable be distributed justly and equally among all classes of our population. These general views, long entertained on this subject, I have deemed it proper to reiterate. It is a subject upon which conflicting interests of sections and occupations are supposed to exist, and a spirit of mutual concession and compromise in adjusting its details should be cherished by every part of our widespread country as the only means of preserving harmony and a cheerful acquiescence of all in the operation of our revenue laws. Our patriotic citizens in every part of the Union will readily submit to the payment of such taxes as shall be needed for the support of their Government, whether in peace or war, if they are so levied as to distribute the burdens as equally as possible among them.

The Republic of Texas has made known her desire to come into our Union, to form a part of our Confederacy and enjoy with us the blessings of liberty secured and guaranteed by our Constitution. Texas was once a part of our country—was unwisely ceded away to a foreign power—is now independent, and possesses an undoubted right to dispose of a part or the whole of her territory and to merge her sovereignty as a separate and independent state in ours. I congratulate my country that by an act of the late Congress of the United States the assent of this Government has given to the reunion, and it only remains for the two countries to agree upon the terms to consummate an object so important to both.

I regard the question of annexation as belonging exclusively to the United States and Texas. They are independent powers competent to contract, and foreign nations have no right to interfere with them or to take exceptions to their reunion. Foreign powers do not seem to appreciate the true character of our Government. Our Union is a confederation of independent States, whose policy is peace with each other and all the world. To enlarge its limits is to extend the dominions of peace over additional territories and increasing millions. The world has nothing to fear from military ambition in our Government. While the Chief Magistrate and the popular branch of Congress are elected for short terms by the suffrages of those millions who must in their own persons bear all the burdens and miseries of war, our Government can not be otherwise than pacific. Foreign powers should therefore look on the annexation of Texas to the United States not as the conquest of a nation seeking to extend her dominions by arms and violence, but as the peaceful acquisition of a territory once her own, by adding another member to our confederation, with the consent of that member, thereby diminishing the chances of war and opening to them new and ever-increasing markets for their products.

To Texas the reunion is important, because the strong protecting arm of our Government would be extended over her, and the vast resources of her fertile soil and genial climate would be speedily developed, while the safety of New Orleans and of our whole southwestern frontier against hostile aggression, as well as the interests of the whole Union, would be promoted by it.

In the earlier stages of our national existence the opinion prevailed with some that our system of confederated States could not operate successfully over an extended territory, and serious objections have at different times been made to the enlargement of our boundaries. These objections were earnestly urged when we acquired Louisiana. Experience has shown that they were not well founded. The title of numerous Indian tribes to vast tracts of country has been extinguished; new States have been admitted into the Union; new Territories have been created and our jurisdiction and laws extended over them. As our population has expanded, the Union has been cemented and strengthened. As our boundaries have been enlarged and our agricultural population has been spread over a large surface, our federative system has acquired additional strength and security. It may well be doubted whether it would not be in greater danger of overthrow if our present population were confined to the comparatively narrow limits of the original thirteen States than it is now that they are sparsely settled over a more expanded territory. It is confidently believed that our system may be safely extended to the utmost bounds of our territorial limits, and that as it shall be extended the bonds of our Union, so far from being weakened, will become stronger.

None can fail to see the danger to our safety and future peace if Texas remains an independent state or becomes an ally or dependency of some foreign nation more powerful than herself. Is there one among our citizens who would not prefer perpetual peace with Texas to occasional wars, which, so often occur between bordering independent nations? Is there one who would not prefer free intercourse with her to high duties on all products and manufactures which enter her ports or cross her frontiers? Is there one who would not prefer an unrestricted communication with her citizens to the frontier obstructions which must occur if she remains out of the Union? Whatever is good or evil in the local institutions of Texas will remain her own whether annexed to the United States or not. None of the present States will be responsible for them any more than they are for the local institutions of each other. They have confederated together for certain specified objects. Upon the same principle that they would refuse to form a perpetual union with Texas because of her local institutions our forefathers would have been prevented from forming our present Union. Perceiving no valid objections to the measure and many reasons for its adoption vitally affecting the peace, the safety, and the prosperity of both countries, I shall on the broad principle which formed the basis and produced the adoption of our Constitution, and not in any narrow spirit of sectional policy, endeavor by all constitutional, honorable, and appropriate means to consummate the expressed will of the people and Government of the United States by the reannexation of Texas to our Union at the earliest practicable period.

Nor will it become in a less degree my duty to assert and maintain by all constitutional means the right of the United States to that portion of our territory which lies beyond the Rocky Mountains. Our title to the country of the Oregon is "clear and unquestionable," and already are our people preparing to perfect that title by occupying it with their wives and children. But eighty years ago our population was confined on the west by the ridge of the Alleghanies. Within that period—within the lifetime, I might say, of some of my hearers—our people, increasing to many millions, have filled the eastern valley of the Mississippi, adventurously ascended the Missouri to its headsprings, and are already engaged in establishing the blessings of self-government in valleys of which the rivers flow to the Pacific. The world beholds the peaceful triumphs of the industry of our emigrants. To us belongs the duty of protecting them adequately wherever they may be upon our soil. The jurisdiction of our laws and the benefits of our republican institutions should be extended over them in the distant regions which they have selected for their homes. The increasing facilities of intercourse will easily bring the States, of which the formation in that part of our territory can not be long delayed, within the sphere of our federative Union. In the meantime every obligation imposed by treaty or conventional stipulations should be sacredly respected.

In the management of our foreign relations it will be my aim to observe a careful respect for the rights of other nations, while our own will be the subject of constant watchfulness. Equal and exact justice should characterize all our intercourse with foreign countries. All alliances having a tendency to jeopard the welfare and honor of our country or sacrifice any one of the national interests will be studiously avoided, and yet no opportunity will be lost to cultivate a favorable understanding with foreign governments by which our navigation and commerce may be extended and the ample products of our fertile soil, as well as the manufactures of our skillful artisans, find a ready market and remunerating prices in foreign markets.

In taking "care that the laws be faithfully executed," a strict performance of duty will be exacted from all public officers. From those officers, especially, who are charged with the collection and disbursement of the public revenue will prompt and rigid accountability be required. Any culpable failure or delay on their part to account for the moneys intrusted to them at the times and in the manner required by law will in every instance terminate the official connection of such defaulting officer with the Government.

Although in our country the Chief Magistrate must almost of necessity be chosen by a party and stand pledged to its principles and measures, yet in his official action he should not be the President of a part only, but of the whole people of the United States. While he executes the laws with an impartial hand, shrinks from no proper responsibility, and faithfully carries out in the executive department of the Government the principles and policy of those who have chosen him, he should not be unmindful that our fellow-citizens who have differed with him in opinion are entitled to the full and free exercise of their opinions and judgments, and that the rights of all are entitled to respect and regard.

Confidently relying upon the aid and assistance of the coordinate departments of the Government in conducting our public affairs, I enter upon the discharge of the high duties which have been assigned me by the people, again humbly supplicating that Divine Being who has watched over and protected our beloved country from its infancy to the present hour to continue His gracious benedictions upon us, that we may continue to be a prosperous and happy people.

FIRST ANNUAL MESSAGE*
December 2, 1845

Polk was satisfied with the progress the nation had made during his first months as President. He carefully prepared his First Annual Message as a record of what he considered to be major accomplishments of his administration. It was a long message, but very provocative. The President reiterated United States claims to the Oregon country, and outlined a unilateral solution to the contested area. His mention of "national honor" has significance; such a term was highly gratifying to most of the expansionist elements of the day.

Perhaps the most important part of the Message was the President's allusion to the Monroe Doctrine. Polk discerned Great Britain and France as having designs on California and North America. The President was led to "reiterate and reaffirm" the noncolonization principle of Monroe's Declaration of 1823.

. . . In pursuance of the joint resolution of Congress "for annexing Texas to the United States," my predecessor, on the 3d day of March, 1845, elected to submit the first and second sections of that resolution to the Republic of Texas as an overture on the part of the United States for her admission as a State into our Union. This election I approved, and accordingly the charge d'affaires of the United States in Texas, under instructions of the 10th of March, 1845, presented these sections of the resolution for the acceptance of that Republic. The executive government, the Congress, and the people of Texas in convention have successively complied with all the terms and conditions of the joint resolutin. A constitution for the government of the States of Texas, formed by a convention of deputies, is herewith laid before Congress. It is well known, also, that the people of Texas at the polls have accepted the terms of annexation and ratified the constitution. I communicate to Congress the correspondence between the Secretary of State and our charge d'affaires in Texas, and also the correspondence of the latter with the authorities of Texas, together with the official documents transmitted by him to his own Government. The terms of annexation which were offered

*James D. Richardson, ed. *Messages and Papers of the Presidents,* Vol. 5, New York, 1897, pp. 2235-2266.

by the United States having been accepted by Texas, the public faith of both parties is solemnly pledged to the compact of their union. Nothing remains to consummate the event but the passage of an act by Congress to admit the State of Texas into the Union upon an equal footing with the original States. Strong reasons exist why this should be done at an early period of the session. It will be observed that by the constitution of Texas the existing government is only continued temporarily till Congress can act, and that the third Monday of the present month is the day appointed for holding the first general election. On that day a governor, a lieutenant-governor, and both branches of the legislature will be chosen by the people. The President of Texas is required, immediately after the receipt of official information that the new States has been admitted into our Union by Congress, to convene the legislature, and upon its meeting the existing government will be superseded and the State government organized. Questions deeply interesting to Texas, in common with the other States, the extension of our revenue laws and judicial system over her people and territory, as well as measures of a local character, will claim the early attention of Congress, and therefore upon every principle of republican government she ought to be represented in that body without unnecessary delay. I can not too earnestly recommend prompt action on this important subject. As soon as the act to admit Texas as a State shall be passed the union of the two Republics will be consummated by their own voluntary consent.

This accession to our territory has been a bloodless achievement. No arm of force has been raised to produce the result. The sword has had no part in the victory. We have not sought to extend our territorial possessions by conquest, or our republican institutions over a reluctant people. It was the deliberate homage of each people to the great principle of our federative union. If we consider the extent of territory involved in the annexation, its prospective influence on America, the means by which it has been accomplished, springing purely from the choice of the people themselves to share the blessings of our nation, the history of the world may be challenged to furnish a parallel. The jurisdiction of the United States, which at the formation of the Federal Constitution was bounded by the St. Marys on the Atlantic, has passed the capes of Florida and been peacefully extended to the Del Norte. In contemplating the grandeur of this event it is not to be forgotten that the result was achieved in despite of the diplomatic interference of European monarchies. Even France, the country which had been our ancient ally, the country which has a common interest with us in maintaining the freedom of the seas, the country which, by the cession of Louisiana, first opened to us access to the Gulf of Mexico, the country with which we have been every year drawing more and more closely the bonds of successful commerce, most unexpectedly, and to our unfeigned regret, took part in an effort to prevent annexation and to impose on Texas, as a condition of the recognition of her independence by Mexico, that she would never join herself to the United States. We may rejoice that the tranquil and pervading influence of the American principle of self-government was sufficient to defeat the purposes of British and French interference, and that the almost unanimous voice of the people of Texas has given to that interference a peaceful and effective rebuke. From this example European Governments may learn how vain diplomatic arts and intrigues must ever prove upon this continent against that system of self-government which seems nature to our soil, and which will ever resist foreign interference.

Toward Texas I do not doubt that a liberal and generous spirit will actuate Congress in all that concerns her interests and prosperity, and that she will never have cause to regret that she has united her "lone star" to our glorious constellation.

I regret to inform you that our relations with Mexico since your last session have not been of the amicable character which it is our desire to cultivate with all foreign nations. On the 6th day of March last the Mexican envoy extraordinary and minister plenipotentiary to the United States made a formal protest in the name of his Government against the joint resolution passed by Congress "for the annexation of Texas to the United States," which he chose to regard as a violation of the rights of Mexico, and in consequence of it he demanded his passports. He was informed that the Government of the United States did not consider this joint resolution as a violation of any of the rights of Mexico, or that it afforded any just cause of offense to his Government; that the Republic of Texas was an independent power, owing no allegiance to Mexico and constituting no part of her territory or rightful sovereignty and jurisdiction. He was also assured that it was the sincere desire of this Government to maintain with that of Mexico relations of peace and good understanding. That functionary, however, notwithstanding these representations and assurances, abruptly terminated his mission and shortly afterwards left the country. Our envoy extraordinary and minister plenipotentiary to Mexico was refused all official intercourse with that Government, and, after remaining several months, by the permission of his own Government he returned to the United States. Thus, by the acts of Mexico, all diplomatic intercourse between the two countries was suspended.

Since that time Mexico has until recently occupied an attitude of hostility toward the United States—has been marshaling and organizing armies, issuing proclamations, and avowing the intention to make war on the United States, either by an open declaration or by invading Texas. Both the Congress and convention of the people of Texas invited this Government to send an army into that territory to protect and defend them against the menaced attack. The moment the terms of annexation offered by the United States were accepted by Texas the latter became so far a part of our own country as to make it our duty to afford such protection and defense. I therefore deemed it proper, as a precautionary measure to order a strong squadron to the coasts of Mexico and to concentrate an efficient military force on the western frontier of Texas. Our Army was ordered to take position in the country between the Nueces and the Del Norte, and to repel any invasion of the Texan territory which might be attempted by the Mexican forces. Our squadron in the Gulf was ordered to cooperate with the Army. But though our Army and Navy were placed in a position to defend our own and the rights of Texas, they were ordered to commit no acts of hostility against Mexico unless she declared war or was herself the aggressor by striking the first blow. The result has been that Mexico has made no aggressive movement, and our military and naval commanders have executed their orders with such discretion that the peace of the two Republics has not been disturbed. Texas had declared her independence and maintained it by her arms for more than nine years. She has had an organized government in successful operation during that period. Her separate existence as an independent state had been recognized by the United States and the principal powers of Europe. Treaties of commerce and navigation had been concluded with her by different nations, and it had become manifest to the whole world that any further attempt on the part of Mexico to conquer her or overthrow her Government would be vain. Even Mexico herself had become satisfied of this fact, and whilst the question of annexation was pending before the people of Texas during the past summer the Government of Mexico, by a formal act, agreed to recognize the independence of Texas on condition that she would not annex herself to any other power. The agreement to acknowledge the independence of Texas, whether with or without this condition, is conclusive against Mexico. The independence of Texas is a fact conceded by Mexico herself, and she had no right or authority to prescribe restrictions as to the form of government which Texas might afterwards choose to assume. But though Mexico can not complain of the United States on account of the annexation of Texas, it is to be regretted that serious causes of misunderstanding between the two countries continue to exist, growing out of unredressed injuries inflicted by the Mexican authorities and people on the persons and property of citizens of the United States through a long series of years. Mexico has admitted these injuries, but has neglected and refused to repair them. Such was the character of the wrongs and such the insults repeatedly offered to American citizens and the American flag by Mexico, in palpable violation of the laws of nations and the treaty between the two countries of the 5th of April, 1831, that they have been repeatedly brought to the notice of Congress by my predecessors. As early as the 6th of February, 1837, the President of the United States declared in a message to Congress that—

"The length of time since some of the injuries have been committed, the repeated and unavailing applications for redress, the wanton character of some of the outrages upon the property and persons of our citizens, upon the officers and flag of the United States, independent or recent insults to this Government and people by the late extraordinary Mexican minister, would justify in the eyes of all nations immediate war. . . ."

The claims which were left undecided by the joint commission, amounting to more than $3,000,000, together with other claims for spoliations on the property of our citizens, were subsequently present to the Mexican Government for payment, and were so far recognized that a treaty providing for their examination and settlement by a joint commission were concluded and signed at Mexico on the 20th day of November, 1843. This treaty was ratified by the United States with certain amendments to which no just exception could have been taken, but it has not yet received the ratification of the Mexican Government. In the meantime our citizens, who suffered great losses—and some of whom have been reduced from affluence to bankruptcy—are without rememdy unless their rights be enforced by their Government. Such a continued and unprovoked series of wrongs could never have been tolerated by the United States had they been committed by one of the principal nations of Europe. Mexico was, however, a neighboring sister republic, which, following our example, had achieved her independence, and for whose success and prosperity all our sympathies were early enlisted. The United States were the first to recognize her independence and to receive her into the family of nations, and have ever been desirous of cultivating with her a good understanding. We have therefore borne the repeated wrongs she has committed with great patience, in the hope that a returning sense of justice would ultimately guide her councils and that we might, if possible, honorably avoid any hostile collision with her. Without the previous authority of Congress the Executive possessed no power to adopt or enforce adequate remedies for the injuries we had suffered, or to do more than to be prepared to repel the threatened aggression on the part of Mexico. After our Army and Navy had remained on the frontier and coasts of Mexico for many weeks without any hostile movement on her part, though her menaces were continued, I deemed it important to put an end, if possible, to this state of things. With this view I caused steps to be taken in the month of September last to ascertain distinctly and in an authentic form what the designs of the Mexican Government were—whether it was their intention to declare war, or invade Texas, or whether they were disposed to adjust and settle in an amicable manner the pending differences between the two countries. On the 9th of November an official answer was received that the Mexican Government consented to renew the diplomatic relations which had been suspended in March last, and for that purpose were willing to accredit a minister from the United States. With a sincere desire to preserve peace and restore relations of good understanding between the two Republics, I waived all ceremony as to the manner of renewing diplomatic intercourse between them, and, assuming the initiative, on the 10th of November a distinguished citizen of Louisiana was appointed envoy extraordinary and minister plenipotentiary to Mexico, clothed with full powers to adjust and definitively settle all pending differences between the two countries, including those of boundary between Mexico and the State of Texas. The minister appointed has set out on his mission and is probably by this time near the Mexican capital. He has been instructed to bring the negotiations with which he is charged to a conclusion at the earliest practicable period, which it is expected will be in time to enable me to communicate the result to Congress during the present session. Until the result is known I forbear to recommend to Congress such ulterior measures of redress for the wrongs and injuries we have so long borne as it would have been proper to make had no such negotiation been instituted. . .

In these attempts to adjust the controversy the parallel of the forty-ninth degree of north latitude had been offered by the United States to Great Britain, and in those of 1818 and 1826, with a further concession of the free navigation of the Columbia River south of that latitude. The parallel of the forty-ninth degree from the Rocky Mountains to its intersection with the northeasternmost branch of the Columbia, and thence down the channel of that river to the sea, had been offered by Great Britain, and with an addition of a small detached territory north of the Columbia. Each of these propositions had been rejected by the parties respectively. In October, 1843, the envoy extraordinary and minister plenipotentiary of the United States in London was authorized to make a similar offer to those made in 1818 and 1826. Thus stood the question when the negotiation was shortly afterwards transferred to Washington, and on the 23d of August, 1844, was formally opened under the direction of my immediate predecessor. Like all the previous negotiations, it was based upon the principles of "compromise," and the avowed purpose of the parties was "to treat the respective claims of the two countries to the Oregon Territory with the view to establish a permanent boundary between them westward of the Rocky Mountains to the Pacific Ocean."

Accordingly, on the 26th of August, 1844, the British plenipotentiary offered to divide the Oregon Territory by the forty-ninth parallel of north latitude from the Rocky Mountains to the point of its intersection with the northeasternmost branch of the Columbia River, and thence down that river to the sea, leaving the free navigation of the river to be enjoyed in common by both parties, the country south of this line to belong to the United States and that north of it to Great Britain. At the same time he proposed in addition to yield to the United States a detached territory north of the Columbia extending along the Pacific and the Straits of Fuca from Bulfinchs Harbor, inclusive, to Hoods Canal, and to make free to the United States any port or ports south of latitude 49° which they might desire, either on the mainland or on Quandra and Vancouvers Island. With the exception of the free ports, this was the same offer which had been made by the British and rejected by the American Government in the negotiations of 1826. This proposition was properly rejected by the American plenipotentiary on the day it was submitted. This was the only proposition of compromise offered by the British plenipotentiary. The proposition on the part of Great Britain having been rejected, the British plenipotentiary requested that a proposal should be made by the United States for "an equitable adjustment of the question." . . .

The proposition thus offered and rejected repeated the offer of the parallel of 49° of north latitude, which had been made by two preceding Administrations, but without proposing to surrender to Great Britain, as they had done, the free navigation of the Columbia River. The right of any foreign power to the free navigation of any of our rivers through the heart of our country was one whhch I was unwilling to concede. It also embraced a provision to make free to Great Britain any port or ports on the cap of Quadra and Vancouvers Island south of this parallel. Had this been a new question, coming under discussion for the first time, this proposition would not have been made. The extraordinary and wholly inadmissible demands of the British Government and the rejection of the proposition made in deference alone to what had been done by my predecessors and the implied obligation which their acts seemed to impose afford satisfactory evidence that no compromise which the United States ought to accept can be effected. With this conviction the proposition of compromise which had been made and rejected was by my direction subsequently withdrawn and our title to the whole Oregon Territory asserted, and, as he believed, maintained by irrefragable facts and arguments.

The civilized world will see in these proceedings a spirit of liberal concession on the part of the United States, and this Government will be relieved from all responsibility which may follow the failure to settle the controversy.

All attempts at compromise having failed, it becomes the duty of Congress to consider what measures it may be proper to adopt for the security and protection of our citizens now inhabiting or who may hereafter inhabit Oregon, and for the maintenance of our just title to that Territory. In adopting measures for this purpose care should be taken that nothing be done to violate the stipulations of the convention of 1827, which is still in force. The faith of treaties, in their letter and spirit, has ever been, and, I trust, will ever be, scrupulously observed by the United States. Under that convention a year's notice is required to be given by either party to the other before the joint occupancy shall terminate and before either can rightfully assert or exercise exclusive jurisdiction over any portion of the territory. This notice it would, in my judgment, be proper to give, and I recommend that provision be made by law for giving it accordingly, and terminating in this manner the convention of the 6th of August, 1827.

It will become proper for Congress to determine what legislation they can in the meantime adopt without violating this convention. Beyond all question the protection of our laws and our jurisdiction, civil and criminal, ought to be immediately extended over our citizens in Oregon. They have had just cause to complain of our long neglect in this particular, and have in consequence been compelled for their own security and protection to establish a provisional government for themselves. Strong in their allegiance and ardent in their attachment to the United States, they have been thus cast upon their own resources.

At the end of the year's notice, should Congress think it proper to make provision for giving that notice, we shall have reached a period when the national rights in Oregon must either be abandoned or firmly maintained. That they can not be abandoned without a sacrifice of both national honor and interest is too clear to admit of doubt.

Oregon is a part of the North American continent, to which, it is confidently affirmed, the title of the United States is the best now in existence. For the grounds on which that title rests I refer you to the correspondence of the late and present Secretary of State with the British plenipotentiary during the negotiation. The British proposition of compromise, which would make the Columbia the line south of 49°, with a trifling addition of detached territory to the United States north of that river, and would leave on the British side two-thirds of the whole Oregon Territory, including the free navigation of the Columbia and all the valuable harbors on the Pacific, can never for a moment be entertained by the United States without an abandonment of their just and clear territorial rights, their own self-respect, and the national honor. For the information of Congress, I communicate herewith the correspondence which took place between the two Governments during the late negotiations.

The rapid extension of our settlements over our territories heretofore unoccupied, the addition of new States to our Confederacy, the expansion of free principles, and our rising greatness as a nation are attracting the attention of the powers of Europe, and lately the doctrine has been broached in some of them of a "balance of power" on this continent to check our advancement. The United States, sincerely desirous of preserving relations of good understanding with all nations, can not in silence permit any European interference on the North American continent, and should any such interference be attempted will be ready to resist it at any and all hazards.

It is well known to the American people and to all nations that this Government has never interfered with the relations subsisting between other governments. We have never made ourselves parties to their wars or their alliances; we have not sought their territories by conquest; we have not mingled with parties in their domestic struggles; and believing our own form of government to be the best, we have never attempted to propogate it by intrigues, by diplomacy, or by force. We may claim on this continent a like exemption from European interference. The nations of America are equally sovereign and independent with those of Europe. They possess the same rights, independent of all foreign interposition, to make war, to conclude peace, and to regulate their internal affairs. The people of the United States can not, therefore, view with indifference attempts of European powers to interfere with the independent action of the nations on this continent. The American system of government is entirely different from that of Europe. Jealousy among the different sovereigns of Europe, lest any of them might become too powerful for the rest, has caused them anxiously to desire the establishment of what they term the "balance of power." It can not be permitted to have any application on the North American continent, and especially to the United States. We must ever maintain the principle that the people of this continent alone have the right to decide their own destiny. Should any portion of them, constituting an independent state, propose to unite themselves with our Confederacy, this will be a question for them and us to determine without any foreign interposition. We can never consent that European powers shall interfere to prevent such a union because it might disturb the "balance of power" which they may desire to maintain upon this continent. Near a quarter of a century ago the principle was distinctly announced to the world in the annual message of one of my predecessors, that—

"The American continents, by the free and independent condition which they have assumed and maintain, are henceforth not to be considered as subjects for future colonization by any European powers."

This principle will apply with greatly increased force should any European power attempt to establish any new colony in North America. In the existing circumstances of the world the present is deemed a proper occasion to reiterate and reaffirm the principle avowed by Mr. Monroe and to state my cordial concurrence in its widsom and sound policy. The reassertion of this principle, especially in reference to North America, is at this day but the promulgation of a policy which no European power should cherish the disposition to resist. Existing rights of every European nation should be respected but it is due alike to our safety and our interests that the efficient protection of our laws should be extended over our whole territorial limits, and that it should be distinctly announced to the whole world as our settled policy that no future European colony or dominion shall with our consent be planted or established on any part of the North American continent. . . .

The late President, in his annual message of December last, recommended an appropriation to satisfy the claims of the Texan Government against the United States, which had been previously adjusted so far as the powers of the Executive extend. These claims arose out of the act of disarming a body of

Texan troops under the command of Major Snively by an officer in the service of the United States, acting under the orders of our Government, and the forcible entry into the custom-house at Bryarlys Landing, on Red River, by certain citizens of the United States and taking away therefrom the goods seized by the collector of the customs as forfeited under the laws of Texas. This was a liquidated debt ascertained to be due to Texas when an independent state. Her acceptance of the terms of annexation proposed by the United States does not discharge or invalidate the claim. I recommend that provision be made for its payment.

The attention of Congress is invited to the importance of making suitable modifications and reductions of the rates of duty imposed by our present tariff laws. The object of imposing duties on imports should be to raise revenue to pay the necessary expenses of Government. Congress may undoubtedly, in the exercise of a sound discretion, discriminate in arranging the rates of duty on different articles, but the discriminations should be within the revenue standard and be made with the view to raise money for the support of Government.

It becomes important to understand distinctly what is meant by a revenue standard the maximum of which should not be exceeded in the rates of duty imposed. It is conceded, and experience proves, that duties may be laid so high as to diminish or prohibit altogether the importation of any given article, and thereby lessen or destroy the revenue which at lower rates would be derived from its importation. Such duties exceed the revenue rates and are not imposed to raise money for the support of Government. If Congress levy a duty for revenue of 1 per cent on a given article, it will produce a given amount of money to the Treasury and will incidentally and necessarily afford protection or advantage to the amount of 1 per cent to the home manufacturer of a similar or like article over the importer. If the duty be raised to 10 per cent, it will produce a greater amount of money and afford greater protection. If it be still raised to 20, 25, or 30 per cent, and if as it is raised the revenue derived from it is found to be increased, the protection or advantage will also be increased; but if it be raised to 31 per cent, and it is found that the revenue produced at that rate is less than at 30 per cent, it ceases to be a revenue duty. The precise point in the ascending scale of duties at which it is ascertained from experience that the revenue is greatest is the maximum rate of duty which can be laid for the *bona fide* purpose of collecting money for the support of Government. To raise the duties higher than that point, and thereby diminish the amount collected, is to levy them for protection merely, and not for revenue. As long, then, as Congress may gradually increase the rate of duty on a given article, and the revenue is increased by such increase of duty, they are within the revenue standard. When they go beyond that point, and as they increase the duties, the revenue is diminished or destroyed; the act ceases to have for its object the raising of money to support Government, but is for protection merely. It does not follow that Congress should levy the highest duty on all articles of import which they will bear within the revenue standard, for such rates would probably produce a much larger amount than the economical administration of the Government would require. Nor does it follow that the duties on all articles should bear the same or a horizontal rate. Some articles will bear a much higher revenue duty than others. Below the maximum of the revenue standard Congress may and ought to discriminate in the rates imposed, taking care so to adjust them on different articles as to produce in the aggregate the amount which, when added to the proceeds of the sales of public lands, may be needed to pay the economical expenses of the Government.

In levying a tariff of duties Congress exercise the taxing power, and for purposes of revenue may select the objects of taxation. They may exempt certain articles altogether and permit their importation free of duty. On others they may impose low duties. In these classes should be embraced such articles of necessity as are in general use, and especially such as are consumed by the laborer and poor as well as by the wealthy citizen. Care should be taken that all the great interests of the country, including manufacturers, agriculture, commerce, navigation, and the mechanic arts, should as far as may be practicable, derive equal advantages from the incidental protection which a just system of revenue duties may afford. Taxation, direct or indirect, is a burden, and it should be so imposed as to operate as equally as may be on all classes in the proportion of their ability to bear it. To make the taxing power an actual benefit to one class necessarily increases the burden of the others beyond their proportion, and would be manifestly unjust. The terms "protection to domestic industry" are of popular import, but they should apply under a just system to all the various branches of industry in our country. The farmer or planter who toils yearly in his fields is engaged in "domestic industry," and is as much entitled to have his labor "protected" as the manufacturer, the man of commerce, the navigator, or the mechanic, who are engaged also in "domestic industry" in their different pursuits. The joint labors of all these classes constitute the aggregate of the "domestic industry" of the nation, and they are equally entitled to the nation's "protection." No one of them can justly claim to be the exclusive recipient of "protection," which can only be afforded by increasing burdens on the "domestic industry" of the others.

If these view be correct, it remains to inquire how far the tariff act of 1842 is consistent with them. That many of the provisions of that act are in violation of the cardinal principles here laid down all must concede. The rates of duty imposed by it on some articles are prohibitory and on others so high as greatly to diminish importations and to produce a less amount of revenue than would be derived from lower rates. They operate as "protection merely" to one branch of "domestic industry" by taxing other branches. . .

The Government in theory knows no distinction of persons or classes, and should not bestow upon some favors and privileges which all others may not enjoy. It was the purpose of its illustrious founders to base the institutions which they reared upon the great and unchanging principles of justice and equity, conscious that if administered in the spirit in which they were conceived they would be felt only by the benefits which they diffused, and would secure for themselves a defense in the hearts of the people more powerful than standing armies and all the means and appliances invented to sustain governments founded in injustice and oppression. . .

In recommending to Congress a reduction of the present rates of duty and a revision and modification of the act of 1842, I am far from entertaining opinions unfriendly to the manufacturers. On the contrary, I desire to see them prosperous as far as they can be so without imposing unequal burdens on other interests. The advantage under any system of indirect taxation, even within the revenue standard, must be in favor of the manufacturing interest, and of this no other interest will complain.

I recommend to Congress the abolition of the minimum principle, or assumed, arbitrary, and false values, and of specific duties, and the substitution in their place of *ad valorem* duties as the fairest and most equitable indirect tax which can be imposed. By the *ad valorem* principles all articles are taxed according to their cost or value, and those which are of inferior quality or of small cost bear only the just proportion of the tax with those which are of superior quality or greater cost. The articles consumed by all are taxed at the same rate. A system of *ad valorem* revenue duties, with proper discriminations and proper guards against frauds in collecting them, it is not doubted will afford ample incidental advantages to the manufacturers and enable them to derive as great profits as can be derived from any other regular business. It is believed that such a system strictly within the revenue standard will place the manufacturing interests on a stable footing and inure to their permanent advantage, while it will as nearly as may be practicable extend to all the great interests of the country the incidental protection which can be afforded by our revenue laws. Such a system, when once firmly established, would be permanent, and not be subject to the constant complaints, agitations, and changes which must ever occur when duties are not laid for revenue, but for the "protection merely" of a favored interest.

In the deliberations of Congress on this subject it is hoped that a spirit of mutual concession and compromise between conflicting interests may prevail, and that the result of their labors may be crowned with the happiest consequences.

By the Constitution of the United States it is provided that "no money shall be drawn from the Treasury but in consequence of appropriations made by law." A public treasury was undoubtedly contemplated and intended to be created, in which the public money should be kept from the period of collection until needed for public uses. In the collection and disbursment of the public money no agencies have ever been employed by law except such as were appointed by the Government, directly responsible to it and under its control. The safe-keeping of the public money should be confided to a public treasury created by law and under like responsibility and control. It is not to be imagined that the framers of the Constitution could have intended that a treasury should be created as a place to deposit and safe-keeping of the public money which was irresponsible to the Government. The first Congress under the Constitution, by the act of the 2d of September, 1789, "to establish the Treasury Department," provided for the appointment of a Treasurer, and made it his duty "to receive and keep the moneys of the United States" and "at all times to submit to the Secretary of the Treasury and the Comptroller, or either of them, the inspection of the moneys in his hands."

That banks, national or State, could not have been intended to be used as a substitute for the Treasury spoken of in the Constitution as keepers of the public money is manifest from the fact that at that time there was no national bank, and but three or four State banks, of limited capital, existed in the country. Their employment as depositories was at first resorted to to a limited extent, but with no avowed intention of continuing them permanently in place of the Treasury of the Constitution. When they were afterwards from time to time employed, it was from motives of supposed convenience. Our experience has shown that when banking corporations have been the keepers of the public money, and been thereby made in effect the Treasury, the Government can have no guaranty that it can command the use of its own money for public purposes. The late Bank of the United States proved to be faithless. The State banks which were afterwards employed were faithless. But a few years ago, with millions of public money in their keeping, the Government was brought almost to bankruptcy and the public credit seriously impaired because of their inability or indisposition to pay on demand to the public creditors in the only currency recognized by the Constitution. Their failure occurred in a period of peace, and great inconvenience and loss were suffered by the public from it. Had the country been involved in a foreign war, that inconvenience and loss would have been much greater, and might have resulted in extreme public calamity. The public money should not be mingled with the private funds of banks or individuals or be used for private purposes. When it is placed in banks for safe-keeping, it is in effect loaned to them without interest, and is loaned by them upon interest to the borrowers from them. The public money is converted into banking capital, and is used and loaned out for the private profit of bank stockholders, and when called for, as was the case in 1837, it may be in the pockets of the borrowers from the banks instead of being in the public Treasury contemplated by the Constitution. The framers of the Constitution could never have intended that the money paid into the Treasury should be thus converted to private use and placed beyond the control of the Government. . .

Entertaining the opinion that "the separation of the moneys of the Government from banking institutions is indispensable for the safety of the funds of the Government and the rights of the people," I recommend to Congress that provision be made by law for such separation, and that a constitutional treasury be created for the safe-keeping of the public money. The constitutional treasury recommended is designed as a secure depository for the public money, without any power to make loans or discounts or to issue any paper whatever as a currency or circulation. I can not doubt that such a treasury as was contemplated by the Constitution should be independent of all banking corporations. The money of the people should be kept in the Treasury of the people created by law, and be in the custody of agents of the people chosen by themselves according to the forms of the Constitution—agents who are directly responsible to the Government, who are under adequate bonds and oaths, and who are subject to severe punishments for any embezzlement, private use, or misapplication of the public funds, and for any failure in other respects to perform their duties. To say that the people or their Government are incompetent or not to be trusted with the custody of their own money in their own Treasury, provided by themselves, but must rely on the presidents, cashiers, and stockholders of banking corporations, not appointed by them nor responsible to them, would be to concede that they are incompetent for self-government.

In recommending the establishment of a constitutional treasury in which the public money shall be kept, I desire that adequate provision be made by law for its safety and that all Executive discretion or control over it shall be removed, except such as may be necessary in directing its disbursement in pursuance of appropriations made by law. . .

MESSAGE TO CONGRESS ON WAR WITH MEXICO*
May 11, 1846

On May 8, 1846 the President received a message that a Mexican force had crossed the Rio Grande. An American scouting mission, under the command of General Zachary Taylor, was ambushed. Polk interpreted the action as an act of war against the United States, and drafted a war message to Congress on May 10, 1846. The war message assumed that a state of war existed, and asked that Congress recognize the status quo. Two days later Congress passed a resolution authorizing Polk to react to the aggression of Mexico. The resolution passed in the House 174-14; in the Senate 40-2.

WASHINGTON, May 11, 1846

To the Senate and House of Representatives:

The existing state of the relations between the United States and Mexico renders it proper that I should bring the subject to the consideration of Congress. In my message at the commencement of your present session the state of these relations, the causes which led to the suspension of diplomatic intercourse between the two countries in March, 1845, and the long-continued and unredressed wrongs and injuries committed by the Mexican Government on the citizens of the United States in their persons and property were briefly set forth.

As the facts and opinions which were then laid before you were carefully considered, I can not better express my present convictions of the condition of affairs up to that time than by referring you to that communication.

. . . In my message at the commencement of the present session I informed you that upon the earnest appeal both of the Congress and convention of Texas I had ordered an efficient military force to take a position "between the Nueces and the Del Norte." This had become necessary to meet a threatened invasion of Texas by the Mexican forces, for which extensive military preparations had been made. The invasion was threatened solely because Texas had determined, in accordance with a solemn resolution of the Con-

*James D. Richardson, ed. *Messages and Papers of the President,* Vol. 5, pp. 2287-2293.

gress of the United States, to annex herself to our Union, and under these circumstances it was plainly our duty to extend our protection over her citizens and soil.

This force was concentrated at Corpus Christi, and remained there until after I had received such information from Mexico as rendered it probable, if not certain, that the Mexican Government would refuse to receive our envoy.

Meantime Texas, by the final action of our Congress, had become an integral part of our Union. The Congress of Texas, by its act of December 19, 1836, had declared the Rio del Norte to be the boundary of that Republic. Its jurisdiction had been extended and exercised beyond the Nueces. The country between that river and the Del Norte had been represented in the Congress and in the convention of Texas, had thus taken part in the act of annexation itself, and is now included within one of our Congressional districts. Our own Congress had, moreover, with great unanimity, by the act approved December 31, 1845, recognized the country beyond the Neuces as a part of our territory by including it within our own revenue system, and a revenue officer to reside within that district has been appointed by and with the advice and consent of the Senate. It became, therefore, of urgent necessity to provide for the defense of that portion of our country. Accordingly, on the 13th of January last instructions were issued to the general in command of these troops to occupy the left bank of the Del Norte. This river, which is the southwestern boundary of the State of Texas, is an exposed froniter. From this quarter invasion was threatened; upon it and in its immediate vicinity, in the judgment of high military experience, are the proper stations for the protecting forces of the Government. In addition to this important consideration, several others occurred to induce this movement. Among these are the facilities afforded by the ports at Brazos Santiago and the mouth of the Del Norte for the reception of supplies by sea, the stronger and more healthful military positions, the convenience for obtaining a ready and a more abundant supply of provisions, water, fuel and forage, and the advantages which are afforded by the Del Norte in forwarding supplies to such posts as may be established in the interior and upon the Indian frontier.

The movement of the troops to the Del Norte was made by the commanding general under positive instructions to abstain from all aggressive acts toward Mexico or Mexican citizens and to regard the relations between that Republic and the United States as peaceful unless she should declare war or commit acts of hostility indicative of a state of war. He was specially directed to protect private property and respect personal rights.

The Army moved from Corpus Christi on the 11th of March, and on the 28th of that month arrived on the left bank of the Del Norte opposite to Matamoras, where it encamped on a commanding position, which has since been strengthened by the erection of fieldworks. A depot has also been established at Point Isabel, near the Brazos Santiago, 30 miles in rear of the encampment. The selection of this position was necessarily confided to the judgement of the general in command.

The Mexican forces at Matamoras assumed a belligerent attitude, and on the 12th of April General Ampudia, then in command, notified General Taylor to break up his camp within twenty-four hours and to retire beyond the Nueces River, and in the event of his failure to comply with these demands announced that arms, and arms alone, must decide the question. But no open act of hostility was committed until the 24th of April. On that day General Arista, who had succeeded to the command of the Mexican forces, communicated to General Taylor that "he considered hostilities commenced and should prosecute them." A party of dragoons of 63 men and officers were on the same day dispatched from the American camp up the Rio del Norte, on its left bank, to ascertain whether the Mexican troops had crossed or were preparing to cross the river, "became engaged with a large body of these troops, and after a short affair, in which some 16 were killed and wounded, appear to have been surrounded and compelled to surrender."

The grievous wrongs perpetrated by Mexico upon our citizens throughout a long period of years remain unredressed, and solemn treaties pledging her public faith for this redress have been disregarded. A government either unable or unwilling to enforce the executiion of such treaties fails to perform one of its plainest duties.

Our commerce with Mexico has been almost annihilated. It was formerly highly beneficial to both nations, but our merchants have been deterred from prosecuting it by the system of outrage and extortion which the Mexican authorities have pursued against them, whilst their appeals through their own Government for indemnity have been made in vain. Our forbearance has gone to such an extreme as to be mistaken in its character. Had we acted with vigor in repelling the insults and redressing the injuries inflicted by Mexico at the commencement, we should doubtless have escaped all the difficulties in which we are now involved.

Instead of this, however, we have been exerting our best efforts to propitiate her good will. Upon the pretext that Texas, a nation as independent as herself, thought proper to unite its destinies with our own she has affected to believe that we have served her rightful territory, and in official proclamations and manifestoes has repeatedly threatened to make war upon us for the purpose of reconquering Texas. In the meantime we have tried every effort at reconciliation. The cup of forbearance had been exhausted even before the recent information from the frontier of the Del Norte. But now, after reiterated menaces, Mexico has passed the boundary of the United States, has invaded our territory and shed American blood upon the American soil. She has proclaimed that hostilities have commenced, and that the two nations are now at war.

As war exists, and, notwithstanding all our efforts to avoid it, exists by the act of Mexico herself, we are called upon by every consideration of duty and patriotism to vindicate with decision the honor, the rights, and the interests of our country.

. . .In further vindication of our rights and defense of our territory, I invoke the prompt action of Congress to recognize the existence of the war, and to place at the disposition of the Executive the means of prosecuting the war with vigor, and thus hastening the restoration of peace. To this end I recommend that authority should be given to call into the public service a large body of volunteers to serve for not less than six or twelve months unless sooner discharged. A volunteer force is beyond question more efficient than any other description of citizen soldiers, and it is not to be doubted that a number far beyond that required would readily rush to the field upon the call of their country. I further recommend that a liberal provision be made for sustaining our entire military force and furnishing it with supplies and munitions of war.

THE OREGON TREATY*
June 15, 1846

After the commencement of the war with Mexico, a spirit of compromise with Great Britain prevailed in the Presidential quarters. President Polk, reversing his previously stated policy of noncompromise, with relation to the Oregon controversy, ordered Secretary of State James Buchanan to present the British proposals before the Senate for its advice. The Senate agreed to Lord Richard Pakenham's compromise proposals, and accepted the Treaty, 41-14.

ARTICLE I.

From the point on the forty-ninth parallel of north latitude where the boundary laid down in existing treaties and conventions between the United States and Great Britain terminates, the line of boundary between the territories of the United States and those of Her Britannic Majesty shall be continued westward along the said forty-ninth parallel of north latitude to the middle of the channel which separates the continent from Vancouver's Island; and thence southerly through the middle of the said channel, and of Fuca's Straits to the Pacific Ocean; provided, however, that the navigation of the whole of the said channel and Straits south of the forty-ninth parallel of north latitude remain free and open to both Parties.

ARTICLE II.

From the point at which the forty-ninth parallel of north latitude shall be found to intersect the great northern branch of the Columbia River, the navigation of the said branch shall be free and open to the Hudson's Bay Company and to all British subjects trading with the same, to the point where the said branch meets the main stream of the Columbia, and thence down the said main stream to the Ocean, with free access into and through the said River or Rivers, it being understood that all the usual portages along the line

*Hunter Miller, ed. *Treaties and other International Acts of the United States of America,* Vol. 5, Washington, D.C., 1937, pp. 3-101.

thus described shall in like manner be free and open. In navigating the said River or Rivers, British subjects with their goods and produce, shall be treated on the same footing as citizens of the United States; it being however always understood that nothing in this article shall be construed as preventing, or intended to prevent, the Government of the United States from making any regulations respecting the navigation of the said river or rivers, not inconsistent with the present treaty.

ARTICLE III.

In the future appropriation of the territory, south of the forty-ninth parallel of north latitude, as provided in the first article of this Treaty, the possessory rights of the Hudson's Bay Company and of all British subjects who may be already in the occupation of land or other property, lawfully acquired within the said Territory, shall be respected.

ARTICLE IV.

The farms, lands, and other property of every description belonging to the Puget's Sound Agricultural Company on the north side of the Columbia River, shall be confirmed to the said Company. In case however the situation of those farms and lands should be considered by the United States to be of public and political importance, and the United States' Government should signify a desire to obtain possession of the whole, or of any part thereof, the property so required shall be transferred to the said Government, at a proper valuation, to be agreed upon between the Parties.

SECOND ANNUAL MESSAGE*
December 8, 1846

The criticism of the Mexican War put the President in a defensive mood. A very long justification, backed by historical evidences, was made for the United States role in the conflict. The following excerpts represent some of Polk's defensive points. The reader, if inclined, may want to read the entire message to discover all the definitive points of view used by Polk's administration. Congressional debate concerning the war was bitter by the end of 1846. The nature of Polk's message was not unrelated to Whig criticism.

. . . The existing war with Mexico was neither desired nor provoked by the United States. On the contrary, all honorable means were resorted to to avert it. After years of endurance of aggravated and unredressed wrongs on our part, Mexico, in violation of solemn treaty stipulations and of every principle of justice recognized by civilian nations, commenced hostilities, and thus by her own act forced the war upon us. Long before the advance of our Army to the left bank of the Rio Grande we had ample cause of war against Mexico, and had the United States resorted to this extremity we might have appealed to the whole civilized world for the justice of our cause. I deem it to be my duty to present to you on the present occasion a condensed review of the injuries we had sustained, of the causes which led to the war, and of its progress since its commencement. This is rendered the more necessary because of the misapprehensions which have to some extent prevailed as to its origin and true character. The war has been represented as unjust and unnecessary and as one of aggression on our part upon a weak and injured enemy. Such erroneous views, though entertained by but few, have been widely and extensively circulated, not only at home, but have been spread throughout Mexico and the whole world. A more effectual means could not have been devised to encourage the enemy and protract the war than to advocate and adhere to their cause, and thus give them "aid and comfort." It is a source of national pride and exultation that the great body of our people have thrown no such obstacles in the way of the Govern-

*James D. Richardson, ed. *The Messages and Papers of the Presidents,* Vol. 5, New York, 1897, pp. 2321-2356.

ment in prosecuting the war successfully, but have shown themselves to be eminently patriotic and ready to vindicate their country's honor and interests at any sacrifice. The alacrity and promptness with which our volunteer forces rushed to the field on their country's call prove not only their patriotism, but their deep conviction that our cause is just.

The wrongs which we have suffered from Mexico almost ever since she became an independent power and the patient endurance with which we have borne them are without a parallel in the history of modern civilized nations. There is reason to believe that if these wrongs had been resented and resisted in the first instance the present war might have been avoided. One outrage, however, permitted to pass with impunity almost necessarily encouraged the perpetration of another, until at last Mexico seemed to attribute to weakness and indecision on our part a forbearance which was the offspring of magnanimity and of a sincere desire to preserve friendly relations with a sister republic.

... Such is the history of the wrongs which we have suffered and patiently endured from Mexico through a long series of years. So far from affording reasonable satisfaction for the injuries and insults we had borne, a great aggravation of them consists in the fact that while the United States, anxious to preserve a good understanding with Mexico, have been constantly but vainly employed in seeking redress for past wrongs, new outrages were constantly occurring, which have continued to increase our causes of complaint and to swell the amount of our demands. While the citizens of the United States were conducting a lawful commerce with Mexico under the guaranty of a treaty of "amity, commerce, and navigation," many of them have suffered all the injuries which would have resulted from open war. This treaty, instead of affording protection to our citizens, has been the means of inviting them into the ports of Mexico that they might be, as they have been in numerous instances, plundered of their property and deprived of their personal liberty if they dared insist on their rights. Had the unlawful seizures of American property and the violation of the personal liberty of our citizens, to say nothing of the insults to our flag, which have occurred in the ports of Mexico taken place on the high seas, they would themselves long since have consituted a state of actual war between the two countries. In so long suffering Mexico to violate her most solemn treaty obligations, plunder our citizens of their property, and imprison their persons without affording them any redress we have failed to perform one of the first and highest duties which every government owes to its citizens, and the consequence has been that many of them have been reduced from a state of affluence to bankruptcy. The proud name of American citizen, which ought to protect all who bear it from insult and injury throughout the world, has afforded no such protection to our citizens in Mexico. We had ample cause for war against Mexico long before the breaking out of hostilities; but even then we forbore to take redress into our own hands until Mexico herself became the aggressor by invading our soil in hostile array and shedding the blood of our citizens.

Such are the grave causes of complaint on the part of the United States against Mexico—causes which existed long before the annexation of Texas to the American Union; and yet, animated by the love of peace and a magnanimous moderation, we did not adopt those measures of redress which under such circumstances are the justified resort of injured nations.

The annexation of Texas to the United States constituted no just cause of offense to Mexico. The pretext that it did so is wholly inconsistent and irreconcilable with well-authenticated facts connected with the revolution by which Texas became independent of Mexico. That this may be the more manifest, it may be proper to advert to the causes and to the history of the principal events of that revolution.

Texas constituted a portion of the ancient Province of Louisiana, ceded to the United States by France in the year 1803. In the year 1819 the United States, by the Florida treaty, ceded to Spain all that part of Louisiana within the present limits of Texas, and Mexico, by the revolution which separated her from Spain and rendered her an independent nation, succeeded to the rights of the mother country over this territory. In the year 1824 Mexico established a federal constitution, under which the Mexican Republic was composed of a number of sovereign States confederated together in a federal union similar to our own. Each of these States had its own executive, legislature, and judiciary, and for all except federal purposes was an independent of the General Government and that of the other States as is Pennsylvania or Virginia under our Constitution. Texas and Coahuila united and formed one of these Mexican States. The State constitution which they adopted, and which was approved by the Mexican Confederacy, asserted that they were "free and independent of the other Mexican United States and of every other power and dominion whatsoever," and proclaimed the great principle of human liberty that "the soverignty of the state resides originally and essentiwly in the general mass of the individuals who compose it." To the Government under this constitution, as well as to that under the federal constitution, the people of Texas owed allegiance.

Emigrants from foreign countries, including the United States, were invited by the colonization laws of the State and of the Federal Government to settle in Texas. Advantageous terms were offered to induce them to leave their own country and become Mexican citizens. This invitation was accepted by many of our citizens in the full faith that in their new home they would be governed by laws enacted by representatives elected by themselves, and that their lives, liberty, and property would be protected by constitutional guaranties similar to those which existed in the Republic they had left. Under a Government thus organized they continued until the year 1835, when a military revolution broke out in the City of Mexico which entirely subverted the federal and State constitutions and placed a military dictator at the head of the Government. By a sweeping decree of a Congress subservient to the will of the Dictator the several State constitutions were abolished and the States themselves converted into mere departments of the central Government. The people of Texas were unwilling to submit to this usurpation. Resistance to such tyranny became a high duty. Texas was fully absolved from all allegiance to the central Government of Mexico from the moment that Government had abolished her State constitution and in its place substituted an arbitrary and despotic central government. Such were the principal causes of the Texan revolution. The people of Texas at once determined upon resistance and flew to arms. In the midst of these important and exciting events, however, they did not omit to place their liberties upon a secure and permanent foundation. They elected members to a convention who in the month of March, 1836, issued a formal declaration that their "political connection with the Mexican nation has forever ended, and that the people of Texas do now constitute a *free, sovereign, and independent Republic,* and are fully invested with all the rights and attributes which properly belong to independent nations." They also adopted for their government a liberal republican constitution. About the same time Santa Anna, then the Dictator of Mexico, invaded Texas with a numerous army for the purpose of subduing her people and enforcing obedience to his arbitrary and despotic Government. On the 21st of April, 1836, he was met by the Texan citizen soldiers, and on that day was achieved by them the memorable victory of San Jacinto, by which they conquered their independence. Considering the numbers engaged on the respective sides, history does not record a more brilliant achievement. Santa Anna himself was among the captives.

In the month of May, 1836, Santa Anna acknowledged by a treaty with the Texan authorities in the most solemn form "the full, entire, and perfect independence of the Republic of Texas." It is true he was then a prisoner of war, but it is equally true that he had failed to reconquer Texas, and had met with signal defeat; that his authority had not been revoked, and that by virtue of this treaty he obtained his personal release. By it hostilities were suspended, and the army which had invaded Texas under his command returned in pursuance of this arrangement unmolested to Mexico.

... The Texas which was ceded to Spain by the Florida treaty of 1819 embraced all the country now claimed by the State of Texas between the Nueces and the Rio Grande. The Republic of Texas always claimed this river as her western boundary, and in her treaty made with Santa Anna in May, 1836, he recognized it as such. By the constitution which Texas adopted in March, 1836, senatorial and representative districts were organized extending west of the Nueces. The Congress of Texas on the 19th of December, 1836, passed

"An act to define the boundaries of the Republic of Texas," in which they declared the Rio Grande from its mouth to its source to be their boundary, and by the said act they extended their "civil and political jurisdiction" over the country up to that boundary. During a period of more than nine years which intervened between the adoption of her constitution and her annexation as one of the States of our Union Texas asserted and exercised many acts of sovereignty and jurisdiction over the territory and inhabitants west of the Nueces. She organized and defined the limits of counties extending to the Rio Grande; she established courts of justice and extended her judicial system over the territory; she established a custom-house and collected duties, and also post-offices and post-roads, in it; she established a land office and issued numerous grants for land within its limits; a senator and a representative residing in it were elected to the Congress of the Republic and served as such before the act of annexation took place. In both the Congress and convention of Texas which gave their assent to the terms of annexation to the United States proposed by our Congress were representatives residing west of the Nueces, who took part inthe act of annexation itself. This was the Texas which by the act of our Congress of the 29th of December, 1845, was admitted as one of the States of the Union. That the Congress of the United States understood the State of Texas which they admitted into the Union to extend beyond the Nueces is apparent from the fact that on the 31st of December, 1845, only two days after the act of admission, they passed a law "to establish a collection district in the State of Texas," by which they created a port of delivery at Corpus Christi, situated west of the Nueces, and being the same point at which the Texas custom-house under the laws of that Republic had been located, and directed that a surveyor to collect the revenue should be appointed for that port by the President, by and with the advice and consent of the Senate. A surveyor was accordingly nominated, and confirmed by the Senate, and has been ever since in the performance of his duties. All these acts of the Republic of Texas and of our Congress preceded the orders for the advance of our Army to the east bank of the Rio Grande. Subsequently Congress passed an act "establishing certain post routes" extending west of the Nueces. The country west of that river now constitutes a part of one of the Congressional districts of Texas and is represented in the House of Representatives. The Senators from that State were chosen by a legislature in which the country west of that river was represented. In view of all these facts it is difficult to conceive upon what ground it can be maintained that in occupying the country west of the Nueces with our Army, with a view solely to its security and defense, we invaded the territory of Mexico. But it would have been still more difficult to justify the Executive, whose duty it is to see that the laws be faithfully executed, if in the face of all these proceedings, both of the Congress of Texas and of the United States, he had assumed the responsibility of yielding up the territory west of the Nueces to

Mexico or of refusing to protect and defend this territory and its inhabitants, including Corpus Christi as well as the remainder of Texas, against the threatened Mexican invasion.

... The movement of our Army to the Rio Grande was made by the commanding general under positive orders to abstain from all aggressive acts toward Mexico and Mexican citizens, and to regard the relations between the two countries as peaceful unless Mexico should declare war or commit acts of hostility indicative of a state of war, and these orders he faithfully executed. Whilst occupying his position on the east bank of the Rio Grande, within the limits of Texas, then recently admitted as one of the States of the Union, the commanding general of the Mexican forces, who in pursuance of the orders of his Government, had collected a large army on the opposite shore of the Rio Grande, crossed the river, invaded our territory, and commenced hostilities by attacking our forces. Thus, after all the injuries which we had received and borne from Mexico, and after she had insultingly rejected a minister sent to her on a mission of peace, and whom she had solemnly agreed to receive, she consummated her long course of outrage against our country by commencing an offensive war and shedding the blood of our citizens on our own soil.

The United States never attempted to acquire Texas by conquest. On the contrary, at an early period after the people of Texas had achieved their independence they sought to be annexed to the United States. At a general election in September, 1836, they decided with great unanimity in favor of "annexation," and in November following the Congress of the Republic authorized the appointment of a minister to bear their request to this Government. This Government, however, having remained neutral between Texas and Mexico during the war between them, and considering it due to the honor of our country and our fair fame among the nations of the earth that we should not at this early period consent to annexation, nor until it should be manifest to the whole world that the reconquest of Texas by Mexico was impossible, refused to accede to the overtures made by Texas. On the 12th of April, 1844, after more than seven years had elapsed since Texas had established her independence, a treaty was concluded for the annexation of that Republic to the United States, which was rejected by the Senate. Finally, on the 1st of March, 1845, Congress passed a joint resolution for annexing her to the United States upon certain preliminary conditions to which her assent was required. The solemnities which characterized the deliberations and conduct of the Government and people of Texas on the deeply interesting questions presented by these resolutions are known to the world. The Congress, the Executive, and the people of Texas, in a convention elected for that purpose, accepted with great unanimity the proposed terms of annexation, and thus consummated on her part the great act of restoring to our Federal Union a vast territory which had been ceded to Spain by the Florida treaty more than a quarter of a century before.

After the joint resolution for the annexation of Texas to the United States had been passed by our Congress the Mexican minister at Washington addressed a note to the Secretary of State, bearing date on the 6th of March, 1845, protesting against it as "an act of aggression the most unjust which can be found recorded in the annals of modern history, namely, that of despoiling a friendly nation like Mexico of a considerable portion of her territory," and protesting against the resolution of annexation as being an act "whereby the Province of Texas, an integral portion of the Mexican territory, is agreed and admitted into the American Union;" and he announced that as a consequence his mission to the United States had terminated, and demanded his passports, which were granted. It was upon the absurd pretext, made by Mexico (herself indebted for her independence to a successful revolution), that the Republic of Texas still continued to be, notwithstanding all that had passed, a Province of Mexico that this step was taken by the Mexican minister.

Every honorable effort has been used by me to avoid the war which followed, but all have proved vain. All our attempts to preserve peace have been met by insult and resistance on the part of Mexico. My efforts to this end commenced in the note of the Secretary of State of the 10th of March, 1845 in answer to that of the Mexican minister. Whilst declining to reopen a discussion which had already been exhausted, and proving again what was known to the whole world, that Texas had long since achieved her independence, the Secretary of State expressed the regret of this Government that Mexico should have taken offense at the resolution of annexation passed by Congress, and gave assurance that our "most strenuous efforts shall be devoted to the amicable adjustment of every cause of complaint between the two Governments and to the cultivation of the kindest and most friendly relations between the sister Republics." That I have acted in the spirit of this assurance will appear from the events which have since occurred. Notwithstanding Mexico had abruptly terminated all diplomatic intercourse with the United States, and ought, therefore, to have been the first to ask for its resumption, yet waiving all ceremony, I embraced the earliest favorable opportunity "to ascertain from the Mexican Government whether they would receive an envoy from the United States intrusted with full power to adjust all the questions in dispute between the two Governments." In September, 1845, I believed the propitious moment for such an overture had arrived. Texas, by the enthusiastic and almost unanimous will of her people, had pronounced in favor of annexation Mexico herself had agreed to acknowledge the independence of Texas, subject to a condition, it is true, which she had no right to impose and no power to enforce. The last lingering hope of Mexico, if she still could have retained any, that Texas would ever again become one of her Provinces, must have been abandoned.

. . . Upon the commencement of hostilities by Mexico upon the United States the indignant ·spirit of the nation was at once aroused. Congress promptly responded to the expectations of the country, and by the act of the 13th of May last recognized the fact that war existed, by the act of Mexico, between the United States and that Republic, and granted the means necessary for its vigorous prosecution. Being involved in a war thus commenced by Mexico, and for the justice of which on our part we may confidently appeal to the whole world, I resolve to prosecute it with the utmost vigor. Accordingly the ports of Mexico on the Gulf and on the Pacific have been placed under blockade and her territory invaded at several important points. The reports from the Departments of War and of the Navy will inform you more in detail of the measures adopted in the emergency in which our country was placed and of the gratifying results which have been accomplished.

The various columns of the Army have performed their duty under great disadvantages with the most distinguished skill and courage. The victories of Palo Alto and Resaca de la Palma and of Monterey, won against greatly superior numbers and against most decided advantages in other respects on the part of the enemy, were brilliant in their execution, and entitle our brave officers and soldiers to the grateful thanks of their country. The nation deplores the loss of the brave officers and men who have gallently fallen while vindicating and defending their country's rights and honor.

. . . The war will continue to be prosecuted with vigor as the best means of securing peace. It is hoped that the decision of the Mexican Congress, to which our last overture has been referred, may result in a speedy and honorable peace. With our experience, however, of the unreasonable course of the Mexican authorities, it is the part of wisdom not to relax in the energy of our military operations until the result is made known. In this view it is deemed important to hold military possession of all the Provinces which have been taken until a definitive treaty of peace shall have been concluded and ratified by the two countries.

The war has not been waged with a view to conquest, but, having been commenced by Mexico, it has been carried into the enemy's country and will be vigorously prosecuted there with a view to obtain an honorable peace, and thereby secure ample indemnity for the expenses of the war, as well as to our much-injured citizens, who hold large pecuniary demands against Mexico.

THIRD ANNUAL MESSAGE*
December 7, 1847

Acrimonious debate over the Mexican War, and how to bring it to an end, raged in Congress. Polk attempted to placate the emotional argument by enumerating the specifics of Nicholas Trist's orders to establish peace with Mexico. Rumors were rife about Trist's refusal to obey Presidential instructions, and the President was reviewing his own relationship with Trist. A hint of the political furor that had arisen is glimpsed in Polk's allusions to Washington's "Farewell Address."

. . . During the past year the most gratifying proofs are presented that our country has been blessed with a widespread and universal prosperity. There has been no period since the Government was founded when all the industrial pursuits of our people have been more successful or when labor in all branches of business has received a fairer or better reward. From our abundance we have been enabled to perform the pleasing duty of furnishing food for the starving millions of less favored countries.

In the enjoyment of the bounties of Providence at home such as have rarely fallen to the lot of any people, it is cause of congratulation that our intercourse with all the powers of the earth except Mexico continues to be of an amicable character.

It has ever been our cherished policy to cultivate peace and good will with all nations, and this policy has been steadily pursued by me.

No change has taken place in our relations with Mexico since the adjournment of the last Congress. The war in which the United States were forced to engage with the Government of the country still continues.

I deem it unnecessary, after the full exposition of them contained in my message of the 11th of May, 1846, and in my annual message at the commencement of the session of Congress in December last, to reiterate the serious causes of complaint which we had against Mexico before she commenced hostilities.

It is sufficient on the present occasion to say that the wanton violation of the rights of person and property of our citizens committed by Mexico, her

*James D. Richardson, ed. *The Messages and Papers of the Presidents,* Vol. 5, New York, 1897, pp. 2382-2414.

repeated acts of bad faith through a long series of years, and her disregard of solemn treaties stipulating for indemnity to our injured citizens not only constituted ample cause of war on our part, but were of such an aggravated character as would have justified us before the whole world in resorting to this extreme remedy. With an anxious desire to avoid a rupture between the two countries, we forbore for years to assert our clear rights by force, and continued to seek redress for the wrongs we had suffered by amicable negotiation in the hope that Mexico might yield to pacific counsels and the demands of justice. In this hope we were disappointed. Our minister of peace sent to Mexico was insultingly rejected. The Mexican Government refused even to hear the terms of adjustment which he was a uthorized to propose, and finally, under wholly unjustifiable pretexts, involved the two countries in war by invading the territory of the State of Texas, striking the first blow, and shedding the blood of our citizens on our own soil.

Though the United States were the aggrieved nation, Mexico commenced the war, and we were compelled in self-defense to repel the invader and to vindicate the national honor and interests by prosecuting it with vigor until we could obtain a just and honorable peace.

. . . The terms of the treaty proposed by the United States were not only just to Mexico, but, considering the character and amount of our claims, the unjustifiable and unprovoked commencement of hostilities by her, the expenses of the war to which we have been subjected, and the success which had attended our arms, were deemed to be of a most liberal character.

The commissioner of the United States was authorized to agree to the establishment of the Rio Grande as the boundary from its entrance into the Gulf to its intersection with the southern boundary of New Mexico, in north latitude about 32°, and to obtain a cession to the United States of the Provinces of New Mexico and the Californias and the privilege of the right of way across the Isthmus of Tehuantepec. The boundary of the Rio Grande and the cession to the United States of New Mexico and Upper California constituted an ultimatum which our commissioner was under no circumstances to yield.

That it might be manifest, not only to Mexico, but to all other nations, that the United States were not disposed to take advantage of a feeble power by insisting upon wresting from her all the other Provinces, including many of her principal towns and cities, which we had conquered and held in our military occupation, but were willing to conclude a treaty in a spirit of liberality, our commissioner was authorized to stipulate for the restoration to Mexico of all our other conquests.

As the territory to be acquired by the boundary proposed might be estimated to be of greater value than a fair equivalent for our just demands, our commissioner was authorized to stipulate for the payment of such additional pecuniary consideration as was deemed reasonable.

The terms of a treaty proposed by the Mexican commissioners were wholly inadmissable. They negotiated as if Mexico were the victorious, and not the vanquished, party. They must have know that their ultimatum could never be accepted. It required the United States to dismember Texas by surrendering to Mexico that part of the territory of that State lying between the Nueces and the Rio Grande, included within her limits by her laws when she was an independent republic, and when she was annexed to the United States and admitted by Congress as one of the States of our Union. It contained no provision for the payment by Mexico of the just claims of our citizens. It required indemnity to Mexican citizens for injuries they may have sustained by our troopes in the prosecution of the war. It demanded the right for Mexico to levy and collect the Mexican tariff of duties on goods imported into her ports while in our military occupation during the war, and the owners of which had paid to officers of the United States the military contributions which had been levied upon them; and it offered to cede to the United States, for a pecuniary consideration, that part of Upper California lying north of latitude 37°. Such were the unreasonable terms proposed by the Mexican commissioners.

The cession to the United States by Mexico of the Provinces of New Mexico and the Californias, as proposed by the commissioner of the United States, it was believed would be more in accordance with the convenience and interests of both nations than any other cession of territory which it was probable Mexico could be induced to make.

It is manifest to all who have observed the actual condition of the Mexican Government for some years past and at present that if these Provinces should be retained by her she could not long continue to hold and govern them. Mexico is too feeble a power to govern these Provinces, lying as they do at a distance of more than 1,000 miles from her capital, and if attempted to be retained by her they would constitute but for a short time even nominally a part of her dominions. This would be especially the case with Upper California.

. . . The Provinces of New Mexico and the Californias are contiguous to the territories of the United States, and if brought under the government of our laws their resources—mineral, agricultural, manufacturing, and commercial—would soon be developed.

Upper California is bounded on the north by our Oregon possessions, and if held by the United States would soon be settled by a hardy, enterprising, and intelligent portion of our population. The Bay of San Francisco and other harbors along the California coast would afford shelter for our Navy, for our numerous whale ships, and other merchant vessels employed in the Pacific Ocean, and would in a short period become the marts of an extensive and profitable commerce with China and other countries of the East.

These advantages, in which the whole commercial world would participate, would at once be secured to the United States by the cession of this
territory; while it is certain that as long as it remains a part of the Mexican
dominions they can be enjoyed neither by Mexico herself nor by any other
nation.

New Mexico is a frontier Province, and has never been of any considerable
value to Mexico. From its locality it is naturally connected with our Western
settlements. The territorial limits of the State of Texas, too, as defined by
her laws before her admission into our Union, embrace all that portion of
New Mexico lying east of the Rio Grande, while Mexico still claims to hold
this territory as a part of her dominions. The adjustment of this question of
boundary is important.

There is another consideration which induced the belief that the Mexican
Government might even desire to place this Province under the protection of
the Government of the United States. Numerous bands of fierce and warlike
savages wander over it and upon its borders. Mexico has been and must continue to be too feeble to restrain them from committing depredations, rob-
beries, and murders, not only upon the inhabitants of New Mexican itself,
but upon those of the other northern States of Mexico. It would be a blessing
to all these northern States to have their citizens protected against them by
the power of the United States. At this moment many Mexicans, principally
females and children, are in captivity among them. If New Mexico were held
and governed by the United States, we could effectually prevent these tribes
from committing such outrages, and compel them to release these captives
and restore them to their families and friends.

In proposing to acquire New Mexico and California, it was known that
but an inconsiderable portion of the Mexican people would be transferred
with them, the country embraced within these Provinces being chiefly an un-
inhabited region.

These were the leading considerations which induced me to authorize the
terms of peace which were proposed to Mexico. They were rejected, and,
negotiations being at an end, hostilities were renewed. An assault was made
by our gallant Army upon the strongly fortified places near the gates of the
City of Mexico and upon the city itself, and after several days of severe conflict the Mexican forces, vastly superior in number to our own, were driven
from the city, and it was occupied by our troops.

Immediately after information was received of the unfavorable result of
the negotiations, believing that his continued presence with the Army could
be productive of no good, I determined to recall our commissioner. A dis-
patch to this effect was transmitted to him on the 6th of October last. The
Mexican Government will be informed of his recall, and that in the existing
state of things I shall not deem it proper to make any further overtures of

peace, but shall be at all times ready to receive and consider any proposals which may be made by Mexico.

Since the liberal proposition of the United States was authorized to be made, in April last, large expenditures have been incurred and the precious blood of many of our patriotic fellow-citizens has been shed in the prosecution of the war. This consideration and the obstinate perserverance of Mexico in protracting the war must influence the terms of peace which it may be deemed proper hereafter to accept.

. . . Had the Government of Mexico acceded to the equitable and liberal terms proposed, that mode of adjustment would have been preferred. Mexico having declined to do this and failed to offer any other terms which could be accepted by the United States, the national honor, no less than the public interests, requires that the war should be prosecuted with increased energy and power until a just and satisfactory peace can be obtained. In the meantime, as Mexico refuses all indemnity, we should adopt measures to indemnify ourselves by appropriating permanently a portion of her territory. Early after the commencement of the war New Mexico and the Californias were taken possession of by our forces. Our military and naval commanders were ordered to conquer and hold them, subject to be disposed of by a treaty of peace.

These Provinces are now in our undisputed occupation, and have been so for many months, all resistance on the part of Mexico having ceased within their limits. I am satisfied that they should never be surrendered to Mexico. Should Congress concur with me in this opinion, and that they should be retained by the United States as indemnity, I can perceive no good reason why the civil jurisdcition and laws of the United States should not at once be extended over them. To wait for a treaty of peace such as we are willing to make, by which our relations toward them would not be changed, can not be good policy; whilst our own interest and that of the people inhabiting them require that a stable, responsible, and free government under our authority should as soon as possible be established over them. Should Congress, therefore, determine to hold these Provinces permanently, and that they shall hereafter be considered as constituent parts of our country, the early establishment of Territorial governments over them will be important for the more perfect protection of persons and property; and I recommend that such Territorial governments be established. It will promote peace and tranquility among the inhabitants, by allaying all apprehension that they may still entertain of being again subjected to the jurisdiction of Mexico. I invite the early and favorable consideration of Congress to this important subject.

Besides New Mexico and the Californias, there are other Mexican Provinces which have been reduced to our possession by conquest. These other

Mexican Provinces are now governed by our military and naval commanders under the general authority which is conferred upon a conqueror by the laws of war. They should continue to be held, as a means of coercing Mexico to accede to just terms of peace. Civil as well as military officers are required to conduct such a government. Adequate compensation, to be drawn from contributions levied on the enemy, should be fixed by law for such officers as may be thus employed. What further provision may become necessary and what final dispostion it may be proper to make of them must depend on the future progress of the war and the course which Mexico may think proper hereafter to pursue.

With the views I entertain I can not favor the policy which has been suggested, either to withdraw our Army altogether or to retire to a designated line and simply hold and defend it. To withdraw our Army altogether from the conquests they have made by deeds of unparalleled bravery, and at the expense of so much blood and treasure, in a just war on our part, and one which, by the act of the enemy, we could not honorably have avoided, would be to degrade the nation in its own estimation and in that of the world. To retire to a line and simply hold and defend it would not terminate the war. On the contrary, it would encourage Mexico to persevere and tend to protract it indefinitely. It is not to be expected that Mexico, after refusing to establish such a line as a permanent boundary when our victorious Army are in possession of her capital and in the heart of her country, would permit us to hold it withour resistance. That she would continue the war, and in the most harassing and annoying forms, there can be no doubt. A border warfare of the most savage character, extending over a long line, would be unceasingly waged. It would require a large army to be kept constantly in the field, stationed at posts and garrisons along such a line, to protect and defend it. The enemy, relieved from the pressure of our arms on his coasts and in the populous parts of the interior, would direct his attention to this line, and, selecting an isolated post for attack, would concentrate his forces upon it. This would be a condition of affairs which the Mexicans, pursuing their favorite system of guerrilla warfare, would probably prefer to any other. Were we to assume a defensive attitude on such a line, all the advantages of such a state of war would be on the side of the enemy. We could levey no contributions upon him, or in any other way make him feel the pressure of the war, but must remain inactive and await his approach, being in constant uncertainty at what point on the line or at what time he might make an assault. He may assemble and organize an overwhelming force in the interior on his own side of the line, and, concealing his purpose, make a sudden assault upon some one of our posts so distant from any other as to prevent the posssbility of timely succor or reenforcements, and in this way our gallant Army would be exposed to the danger of being cut off in detail; or if by their unequaled bravery and prowess everywhere exhibited during this war they should repulse the enemy, their numbers stationed at any one post may be too small to pursue him. If the enemy be repulsed in one attack, he would having nothing to do but to retreat to his own side of the line, and, being in no fear of a pursuing army, may reenforce himself at leisure for another attack on the same or some other post. He may, too, cross the line between our posts, make rapid incursions into the country which we hold, murder the inhabitants, commit depredations on them, and then retreat to the interior before a sufficient force can be concentrated to pursue him. Such would probably be the harassing character of a mere defensive war on our part. If our forces when attacked, or threatened with attack, be permitted to cross the line, drive back the enemy, and conquer him, this would be again to invade the enemy's country after having lost all the advantages of the conquests we have already made by having voluntarily abandoned them. To hold such a line successfully and in security it is far from being certain that it would not require as large an army as would be necessary to hold all the conquests we have already made and to continue the prosecution of the war in the heart of the enemy's country. It is also far from being certain that the expenses of the war would be diminished by such a policy.

I am persuaded that the best means of vindicating the national honor and interest and of bringing the war to an honorable close will be to prosecute it with increased energy and power in the vital parts of the enemy's country.

In my annual message to Congress of December last I declared that—

"The war has not been waged with a view to conquest, but, having been commenced by Mexico, it has been carried into the enemy's country and will be vigorously prosecuted there with a view to obtain an honorable peace, and thereby secure ample indemnity for the expenses of the war, as well as to our much-injured citizens, who hold large pecuniary demands against Mexico."

Such, in my judgment, continues to be our true policy; indeed, the only policy which will probably secure a permanent peace.

It has never been contemplated by me, as an object of the war, to make a permanent conquest of the Republic of Mexico or to annihilate her separate existence as an independent nation. On the contarry, it has ever been my desire that she should maintain her nationality, and under a good government adapted to her condition be a free, independent, and prosperous Republic. The United States were the first among the nations to recognize her independence, and have always desired to be on terms of amity and good neighborhood with her. This she would not suffer. By her own conduct we have been compelled to engage in the present war. In its prosecution we seek not her overthrow as a nation, but in vindicating our national honor we seek to obtain redress for the wrongs she has done us and indemnity for our just demands against her. We demand an honorable peace, and that peace must bring with it indemnity for the past and security for the future. Hitherto Mexico has refused all accommodation by which such a peace could be obtained.

Whilst our armies have advanced from victory to victory from the commencement of the war, it has always been with the olive branch of peace in their hands, and it has been in the power of Mexico at every step to arrest hostilities by accepting it.

. . . Mexico is our near neighbor, and her boundaries are coterminous with our own through the whole extent across the North American continent, from ocean to ocean. Both politically and commercially we have the deepest interest in her regeneration and prosperity. Indeed, it is impossible that, with any just regard to our own safety, we can ever become indifferent to her fate.

It may be that the Mexican Government and people have misconstrued or misunderstood our forbearance and our objects in desiring to conclude an amicable adjustment of the existing differences between the two countries. They may have supposed that we would submit to terms degrading to the nation, or they may have drawn false inferences from the supposed division of opinion in the United States on the subject of the war, and may have calculated to gain much by protracting it, and, indeed, that we might ultimately abandon it altogether without insisting on any indemnity, territorial or otherwise. Whatever may be the false impressions under which they have acted, the adoption and prosecution of the energetic policy proposed must soon undeceive them.

. . . It has been my constant effort to maintain and cultivate the most intimate relations of friendship with all the independent powers of South America, and this policy has been attended with the happiest results. It is true that the settlement and payment of many just claims of American citizens against these nations have been long delayed. The peculiar position in which they have been placed and the desire on the part of my predecessors as well as myself to grant them the utmost indulgence have hitherto prevented these claims from being urged in a manner demanded by strict justice. The time has arrived when they ought to be finally adjusted and liquidated, and efforts are now making for that purpose.

All the public lands which had been surveyed and were ready for market have been proclaimed for sale during the past year. The quantity offered and to be offered for sale under proclamations issued since the 1st of January last amounts to 9,138,531 acres. The prosperity of the Western States and Territories in which these lands lie will be advanced by their speedy sale. By withholding them from market their growth and increase of population would be retarded, while thousands of our enterprising and meritorious frontier population would be deprived of the opportunity of securing freeholds for themselves and their families. But in addition to the general considerations which rendered the early sale of these lands proper, it was a leading object at this time to derive as large a sum as possible from this source, and thus diminish by that amount the public loan rendered necessary by the existence of a foreign war.

It is estimated that not less than 10,000,000 acres of the public lands will be surveyed and be in a condition to be proclaimed for sale during the year 1848.

In my last annual message I presented the reasons which in my judgement rendered it proper to graduate and reduce the price of such of the public lands as have remained unsold for long periods after they had been offered for sale at public auction.

Many millions of acres of public lands lying within the limits of several of the Western States have been offered in the market and been subject to sale at private entry for more than twenty years and large quantities for more than thirty years at the lowest price prescribed by the existing laws, and it has been found that they will not command that price. They must remain unsold and uncultivated for an indefinite period unless the price demanded for them by the Government shall be reduced. No satisfactory reason is perceived why they should be longer held at rates above their real value. At the present period an additional reason exists for adopting the measure recommended. When the country is engaged in a foreign war, and we must necessarily resort to loans, it would seem to be the dictate of wisdom that we should avail ourselves of all our resources and thus limit the amount of the public indebtedness to the lowest possible sum.

I recommend that the existing laws on the subject of preemption rights be amended and modified so as to operate prospectively and to embrace all who may settle upon the public lands and make improvements upon them, before they are surveyed as well as afterwards, in all cases where such settlements may be made after the Indian title shall have been extinguished.

If the right of preemption be thus extended, it will embrace a large and meritorious class of our citizens. It will increase the number of small freeholders upon our borders, who will be enabled thereby to educate their children and otherwise improve their condition, while they will be found at all times, as they have ever proved themselves to be in the hour of danger to their country, among our hardiest and best volunteer soldiers, ever ready to attend to their services in cases of emergencies and among the last to leave the field as long as an enemy remains to be encountered. Such a policy will also impress these patriotic pioneer emigrants with deeper feelings of gratitude for the parental care of their Government, when they find their dearest interests secured to them by the permanent laws of the land and that they are no longer in danger of losing their homes and hard-earned improvements by being brought into competition with a more wealthy class of purchasers at the land sales.

I recommend also that grants, upon liberal terms, of limited quantities of the public lands be made to all citizens of the United States who have emigrated, or may hereafter within a prescribed period emigrate, to Oregon and settle upon them. These hardy and adventurous citizens, who have encountered the dangers and privations of a long and toilsome journey, and have at length found an abiding place for themselves and their families upon the utmost verge of our western limits, should be secured in the homes which they have improved by their labor.

In view of the existing state of our country, I trust it may not be inappropriate, in closing this communication, to call to mind the words of wisdom and admonition of the first and most illustrious of my predecessors in his Farewell Address to his countrymen.

That greatest and best of men, who served his country so long and loved it so much, foresaw with "serious concern" the danger to our Union of "characterizing parties by *geographical* discriminations—*Northern* and *Southern, Atlantic* and *Western*—whence designing men may endeavor to excite a belief that there is a real difference of local interests and views," and warned his countrymen against it.

So deep and solemn was his conviction of the importance of the Union and of preserving harmony between its different parts, that he declared to his countrymen in that address:

"It is of infinite moment that you should properly estimate the immense value of your national union to your collective and individual happiness; that you should cherish a cordial, habitual, and immovable attachment to it; accustoming yourselves to think and speak of it as of the palladium of your political safety and prosperity; watching for its preservation with jealous anxiety; discountenancing whatever may suggest even a suspicion that it can in any event be abandoned, and indignantly frowning upon the first dawning of every attempt to alienate any portion of our country from the rest or to enfeeble the sacred ties which now link together the various parts."

After the lapse of half a century these admonitions of Washington fall upon us with all the force of truth. It *is* difficult to estimate the "immense value" of our glorious Union of confederated States, to which we are so much indebted for our growth in population and wealth and for all that constitutes us a great and a happy nation. How unimportant are all our differences of opinion upon minor questions of public policy compared with its preservation, and how scrupulously should we avoid all agitating topics which may tend to distract and divide us into contending parties, separated by geographical lines, whereby it may be weakened or endangered.

Invoking the blessing of the Almighty Ruler of the Universe upon your deliberations, it will be my highest duty, no less than my sincere pleasure, to cooperate with you in all measures which may tend to promote the honor and enduring welfare of our common country.

TREATY OF GUADALUPE-HIDALGO*
Ratified March 10, 1848

Although strongly disapproving of the independent role played by Nicholas Trist in making the peace treaty with Mexico, Polk nonetheless felt it would be wise to accept it. He knew the political passions of the day would only be further aroused, and a treaty on broader terms would probably not be passed in the long run. The Treaty of Guadalupe-Hidalgo, signed in Mexico on February 2, was ratified by the Senate, 38-14, on March 10, 1848, and by the Mexican Congress on May 25. Ratifications were exchanged on May 30, and the treaty proclaimed in effect by Polk on July 4, 1848.

ARTICLE I.

. . . There shall be firm and universal peace between the United States of America and the Mexican Republic, and between their respective countries, territories, cities, towns and people, without exception of places or persons.

ARTICLE II.

Immediately upon the signature of this Treaty, a convention shall be entered into between a Commissioner or Commissioners appointed by the General in Chief

ARTICLE V.

. . . The Boundary line between the two Republics shall commence in the Gulf of Mexico, three leagues from land, opposite the mouth of the Rio Grande, otherwise called Rio Bravo del Norte, or opposite the mouth of it's deepest branch, if it should have more than one branch emptying directly into the sea; from thence, up the middle of that river, following the deepest channel, where it has more than one, to the point where it strikes the southern boundary of New Mexico; thence, westwardly, along the whole southern boundary of New Mexico (which runs north of the town called *Paso*) to

*Hunter Miller, ed. *Treaties and Other International Acts of the United States of America,* Vol. 5, Washington, D.C., 1937, pp. 207-428.

it's western termination; thence, northward, along the western line of New Mexico, until it intersects the first branch of the river Gila; (or it it should not intersect any branch of that river, then, to the point on the said line nearest to such branch, and thence in a direct line to the same;) thence down the middle of the said branch and of the said river, until it empties into the Rio Colorado; thence, across the Rio Colorado, following the division line between Upper and Lower California, to the Pacific Ocean.

ARTICLE VII.

. . . The river Gila, and the part of the Rio Bravo del Norte lying below the southern boundary of New Mexico, being, agreeably to the fifth Article, divided in the middle between the two Republics, the navigation of the Gila and of the Bravo below said boundary shall be free and common to the vessels and citizens of both countries; and neither shall, without the consent of the other, construct any work that may impede or interrupt, in whole or in part, the exercise of this right: not even for the purpose of favouring new methods of navigation. Nor shall any tax or contribution, under any denomination or title, be levied upon vessels or persons navigating the same, or upon merchandise or effects transported thereon, except in the case of landing upon one of their shores. If, for the purpose of making the said rivers navigable, or for maintaining them in such state, it should be necessary or advantageous to establish any tax or contribution, this shall not be done without the consent of both Governments.

The stipulations contained in the present Article shall not impair the the territorial rights of either Republic, within it's established limits.

ARTICLE VIII.

Mexicans now established in territories previously belonging to Mexico, and which remain for the future within the limits of the United States, as defined by the present treaty, shall be free to continue where they now reside, or to remove at any time to the Mexican Republic, retaining the property which they possess in the said territories, or disposing thereof, and removing the proceeds wherever they please; without their being subjected, on this account, to any contribution, tax or change whatever.

Those who shall prefer to remain in the said territories, may either retain the title and rights of Mexican citizens, or acquire those of citizens of the United States. But they shall be under the obligatiin to make their election within one year from the date of the exchange of ratifications of this treaty: and those who shall remain in the said territories, after the expiration of that year, without having declared their intention to retain the character of Mexicans, shall be considered to have elected to become citizens of the United States.

In the said territories, property of every kind, now belonging to Mexicans, not established there, shall be inviolably respected. The present owners, the heirs of these, and all Mexicans who may hereafter acquire said property by contract, shall enjoy with respect to it, guaranties equally ample as if the same belonged to citizens of the United States.

ARTICLE XIII.

. . . The United States engage moreover, to assume and pay to the claimants all the amounts now due them, and those hereafter to become due, and reason of the claims already liquidated and decided against the Mexican Republic, under the conventions between the two Republics severally concluded on the eleventh day of April eighteen hundred and thirty-nine, and on the thirtieth day of January eighteen hundred and forty three: so that the Mexican Republic shall be absolutely exempt for the future, from all expense whatever on account of the said claims.

ARTICLE XIV.

The United States do furthermore discharge the Mexican Republic from all claims of citizens of the United States, not heretofore decided against the Mexican Government, which may have arisen previously to the date of the signature of this treaty: which discharge shall be final and perpetual, whether the said claims be rejected or be allowed by the Board of Commissioners provided for in the following Article, and whatever shall be the total amount of those allowed.

ARTICLE XV.

The United States, exonerating Mexico from all demands on account of the claims of their citizens mentioned in the preceding Article, and considering them entirely and forever cancelled, whatever their amount may be, undertake to make satisfaction for the same, to an amount not exceeding three and one quarter millions of Dollars. To ascertain the validity and amount of those claims, a Board of Commissioners shall be established by the Government of the United States, whose awards shall be final and conclusive: provided that in deciding upon the validity of each claim, the board shall be guided and governed by the principles and rules of decision prescribed by the first and fifth Articles of the unratified convention, concluded at the City of Mexico on the twentieth day of November, one thousand eight hundred and forty-three; and in no case shall an award be made in favour of any claim not embraced by these principles and rules.

ARTICLE XXI.

. . . If unhappily any disagreement should hereafter arise between the Governments of the two Republics, whether with respect to the interpretation or any stipulation in this treaty, or with respect to any other particular concerning the political or commercial relations of the two Nations, the said Governments, in the name of those Nations, do promise to each other, that they will endeavour in the most sincere and earnest manner, to settle the differences so arising, and to preserve the state of peace and friendship, in which the two countries are now placing themselves: using, for this end, mutual representations and pacific negotiations. And, if by these means, they should not be enabled to come to an agreement, a resort shall not, on this account, be had to reprisals, aggression or hostility of any kind, by the one Republic against the other, until the Government of that which deems itself aggrieved, shall have maturely considered, in the spirit of peace and good neighbourship, whether it would not be better that such difference should be settled by the arbitration of Commissioners appointed on each side, or by that of a friendly nation. And should such course be proposed by either party, it shall be acceded to by the other, unless deemed by it altogether incompatible with the nature of the difference, or the circumstances of the case.

FOURTH ANNUAL MESSAGE*
December 5, 1848

Polk's last address to Congress was an occasion for self-gratification for the President. He had accomplished his mission for the nation; his most desired goals for his administration had been met. This message was widely reprinted. The section mentioning the discovery of gold in California had much to do with the "rush of '49." A masterful defense of Presidential authority, at the end of his address, reinforced the Jacksonian interpretation of the importance of strong executive leadership.

Within less than four years the annexation of Texas to the Union has been consummated; all conflicting title to the Oregon Territory south of the forty-ninth degree of north latitude, being all that was insisted on by any of my predecessors, has been adjusted, and New Mexico and Upper California have been acquired by treaty. The area of these several Territories, according to a report carefully prepared by the Commissioner of the General Land Office from the most authentic information in his possession, and which is herewith trransmitted, contains 1,193,061 square miles, or 763,559,040 acres; while the area of the remaining twenty-nine States and the territory not yet organized into States east of the Rocky Mountains contains 2,059,513 square miles, or 1,318,126,058 acres. These estimates show that the territories recently acquired, and over which our exclusive jurisdiction and dominion have been extended, constitute a country more than half as large as all that which was held by the United States before their acquisition. If Oregon be excluded from the estimate, there will still remain within the limits of Texas, New Mexico, and California 851,598 square miles, or 545,012,720 acres, being an addition equal to more than one-third of all the territory owned by the United States before their acquisition, and, including Oregon, nearly as great an extent of territory as the whole of Europe, Russia only excepted. The Mississippi, so lately the frontier of our country, is now only its center. With the addition of the late acquisitions, the United States are now estimated to be nearly as large as the whole of Europe. It is estimated by the Superintendent of the Coast Survey in the accompanying report that

*James D. Richardson, ed. *Messages and Papers of the Presidents,* Vol. 6, New York, 1897, pp. 2479-2528.

the extent of the seacoast of Texas on the Gulf of Mexico is upward of 400 miles; of the coast of Upper California on the Pacific, of 970 miles, and of Oregon, including the Straits of Fuca, 650 miles, making the whole extent of seacoast on the Pacific 1,620 miles and the whole extent on both the Pacific and the Gulf of Mexico 2,020 miles. The length of the coast on the Atlantic from the northern limits of the United States around the capes of Florida to the Sabine, on the eastern boundary of Texas, is estimated to be 3,100 miles; so that the addition of seacoast, including Oregon, is very nearly two-thirds as great as all we possessed before, and, exluding Oregon, is an addition of 1,370 miles, being nearly equal to one-half of the extent of coast which we possessed before these acquisitions. We have now three great maritime fronts—on the Atlantic, the Gulf of Mexico, and the Pacific—making in the whole an extent of seacoast exceeding 5,000 miles. This is the extent of the seacoast of the United States, not including bays, sounds, and small irregularities of the main shore and of the sea islands. If these be included, the length of the shore line of coast, as estimated by the Superintendent of the Coast Survey in his report, would be 33,063 miles.

It would be difficult to calculate the value of these immense additions to our territorial possessions. Texas, lying contiguous to the western boundary of Louisiana, embracing withint its limits a part of the navigable tributary waters of the Mississippi and an extensive seacoast, could not long have remained in the hands of a foreign power without endangering the peace of our southwestern frontier. Her products in the vicinity of the tributaries of the Mississippi must have sought a market through these streams, running into and through our territory, and the danger of irritation and collision of interests between Texas as a foreign state and ourselves would have been imminent, while the embarrassments in the commercial intercourse between them must have been constant and unavoidable. Had Texas fallen into the hands or under the influence and control of a strong maritime or military foreign power, as she might have done, these dangers would have been still greater. They have been avoided by her voluntary and peaceful annexation to the United States. Texas, from her position, was a natuarl and almost indispensable part of our territories. Fortunately, she has been restored to our country, and now constitutes one of the States of our Confederacy, "upon an equal footing with the original States." The salubrity of climate, the fertility of soil, peculiarly adapted to the production of some of our most valuable staple commodities, and her commercial advantages must soon make her one of our most populous States.

New Mexico, though situated in the interior and without a seacoast, is known to contain much fertile land, to abound in rich mines of the precious metals, and to be capable of sustaining a large population. From its position it is the intermediate and connecting territory between our settlements and our possessions in Texas and those on the Pacific Coast.

Upper California, irrespective of the vast mineral wealth recently developed there, holds at this day, in point of value and importance, to the rest of the Union the same relation that Louisiana did when that fine territory was acquired from France forty-five years ago. Extending nearly ten degrees of latitude along the Pacific, and embracing the only safe and commodious harbors on that coast for many hundred miles, with a temperate climate and an extensive interior of fertile lands, it is scarcely possible to estimate its wealth until it shall be brought under the government of our laws and its resources fully developed. From its position it must command the rich commerce of China, of Asia, of the islands of the Pacific, of western Mexico, of Central America, the South American States, and of the Russian possessions bordering on that ocean. A great emporium will doubtless speedily arise on the California coast which may be destined to rival in importance New Orleans itself. The depot of the vast commerce which must exist on the Pacific will probably be at some point on the Bay of San Francisco, and will occupy the same relation to the whole western coast of that ocean as New Orleans does to the valley of the Mississippi and the Gulf of Mexico. To this depot our numerous whale ships will resort with their cargoes to trade, refit, and obtain supplies. This of itself will largely contribute to build up a city, which would soon become the center of a great and rapidly increasing commerce. Situated on a safe harbor, sufficiently capacious for all the navies as well as the marine of the world, and convenient to excellent timber for shipbuilding, owned by the United States, it must become our great Western naval depot.

It was known that mines of the precious metals existed to a considerable extent in California at the time of its acquisition. Recent discoveries render it probable that these mines are more extensive and valuable than was anticipated. The accounts of the abundance of gold in that territory are of such an extraordinary character as would scarcely command belief were they not corroborated by the authentic reports of officers in the public service who have visited the mineral district and derived the facts which they detail from personal observation. Reluctant to credit the reports in general circulation as to the quantity of gold, the officer commanding our forces in California visited the mineral district in July last for the purpose of obtaining accurate information on the subject. His report to the War Department of the result of his examination and the facts obtained on the spot is herewith laid before Congress. When he visited the country there were about 4,000 persons engaged in collecting gold. There is every reason to believe that the number of persons so employed has since been augmented. The explorations already made warrant the belief that the supply is very large and the gold is found at various places in an extensive district of country.

Information received from officers of the Navy and other sources, though not so full and minute, confirms the accounts of the commander of our military force in California. It appears also from these reports that mines of quicksilver are found in the vicinity of the gold region. One of them is now being worked, and is believed to be among the most productive in the world.

The effects produced by the discovery of these rich mineral deposits and the success which has attended the labors of those who have resorted to them have produced a surprising change in the state of affairs in California. Labor commands a most exorbitant price, and all other pursuits but that of searching for the precious metals are abandoned. Nearly the whole of the male population of the country have gone to the gold districts. Ships arriving on the coast are deserted by their crews and their voyages suspended for want of sailors. Our commanding officer there entertains apprehensions that soldiers can not be kept in the public service without a large increase of pay. Desertions in his command have become frequent, and he recommends that those who shall withstand the strong temptation and remain faithful should be rewarded.

. . . The acquisition of California and New Mexico, the settlement of the Oregon boundary, and the annexation of Texas, extending to the Rio Grande, are results which, combined, are of greater consequence and will add more to the strength and wealth of the nation than any which have preceded them since the adoption of the Constitution.

. . . The question is believed to be rather abstract than practical, whether slavery ever can or would exist in any portion of the acquired territory even if it were left to the option of the slaveholding States themselves. From the nature of the climate and productions in much the larger portion of it it is certain it could never exist, and in the remainder the probabilities are it would not. But however this may be, the question, involving, as it does, a principle of equality of rights of the separate and several States as equal co-partners in the Confederacy, should not be disregarded.

In organizing governments over these territories no duty imposed on Congress by the Constitution requires that they should legislate on the subject of slavery, while their power to do so is not only seriously questioned, but denied by many of the soundest expounders of that instrument. Whether Congress shall legislate or not, the people of the acquired territories, when assembled in convention to form State constitutions, will possess the sole and exclusive power to determine for themselves whether slavery shall or shall not exist within their limits. If Congress shall abstain from interfering with the question, the people of these territories will be left free to adjust it as they may think proper when they apply for admission as States into the Union. No enactment of Congress could restrain the people of any of the sovereign States of the Union, old or new, North or South, slaveholding or nonslaveholding, from determining the character of their own domestic institutions as they may deem wise and proper. Any and all the States possess this right, and Congress can not deprive them of it. The people of

Georgia might if they chose so alter their constitution as to abolish slavery within its limits, and the people of Vermont might so alter their constitution as to admit slavery within its limits. Both States would possess the right, though, as all know, it is not probable that either would exert it.

It is fortunate for the peace and harmony of the Union that this question is in its nature temporary and can only continue for the brief period which will intervene before California and New Mexico may be admitted as States into the Union. From the tide of population now flowing into them it is highly probable that this will soon occur.

Considering the several States and the citizens of the several States as equals and entitled to equal rights under the Constitution, if this were an original question it might well be insisted on that the principle of noninterference is the true doctrine and that Congress could not, in the absence of any express grant of power, interfere with their relative rights. Upon a great emergency, however, and under menacing dangers to the Union, the Missouri compromise line in respect to slavery was adopted. The same line was extended farther west in the acquisition of Texas. After an acquiescence of nearly thirty years in the principle of compromise recognized and established by these acts, and to avoid the danger to the Union which might follow if it were not disregarded, I have heretofore expressed the opinion that that line of compromise should be extended on the parallel of 36° 30′ from the western boundary of Texas, where it now terminates, to the Pacific Ocean. This is the middle ground of compromise, upon which the different sections of the Union may meet, as they have heretofore met. If this be done, it is confidently believed a large majority of the people of every section of the country, however widely their abstract opinions on the subject of slavery may differ, would cheerfully and patriotically acquiesce in it, and peace and harmony would again fill our borders.

The restriction north of the line was only yielded to in the case of Missouri and Texas upon a principle of compromise, made necessary for the sake of preserving the harmony and possibly the existence of the Union.

It was upon these considerations that at the close of your last session I gave my sanction to the principle of the Missouri compromise line by approving and signing the bill to establish "the Territorial government of Oregon." From a sincere desire to preserve the harmony of the Union, and in deference for the acts of my predecessors, I felt constrained to yield my acquiescence to the extent to which they had gone in compromising this delicate and dangerous question. But if Congress shall now reverse the decision by which the Missouri compromise was effected, and shall propose to extend the restriction over the whole territory, south as well as north of the parallel of 36° 30′, it will cease to be a compromise, and must be regarded as an original question.

If Congress, instead of observing the course of noninterference, leaving the adoption of their own domestic institutions to the people who may in-habit these territories, or if, instead of extending the Missouri compromise line to the Pacific, shall prefer to submit the legal and constitutional ques-tions which may arise to the decision of the judicial tribunals, as was pro-posed in a bill which passed the Senate at your last session, and adjustment may be effected in this mode. If the whole subject be referred to the judiciary, all parts of the Union should cheerfully acquiesce in the final decision of the tribunal created by the Constitution for the settlement of all questions which may arise under the Constitution, treaties, and laws of the United States.

Congress is earnestly invoked, for the sake of the Union, its harmony, and our continued prosperity as a nation, to adjust at its present session this, the only dangerous question which lies in our path, if not in some one of the modes suggested, in some other which may be satisfactory.

... The preservation of the Constitution from infraction is the President's highest duty. He is bound to discharge that duty at whatever hazard of in-curring the displeasure of those who may differ with him in opinion. He is bound to discharge it as well by his obligations to the people who have clothed him with his exalted trust as by his oath of office, which he may not disregard. Nor are the obligations of the President in any degree lessened by the prevalence of views different from his own in one or both Houses of Congress. It is not alone hasty and inconsiderate legislation that he is re-quired to check; but if at any time Congress shall, after apparently full deliberation, resolve on measures which he deems subversive of the Constitu-tion or of the vital interests of the country, it is his solemn duty to stand in the breach and resist them. The President is bound to approve or disapprove every bill which passes Congress and is presented to him for his signature. The Constitution makes this his duty, and he can not escape it if he would. He has no election. In deciding upon any bill presented to him he must exer-cise his own best judgment. If he can not approve, the Constitution com-mands him to return the bill to the House in which it originated with his ob-jections, and if he fail to do this within ten days (Sundays excepted) it shall become a law without his signature. Right or wrong, he may be overruled by a vote of two-thirds of each House, and in that event the bill becomes a law without his sanction. If his objections be not thus overruled, the subject is only postponed, and is referred to the States and the people for their con-sideration and decision. The President's power is negative merely, and not affirmative. He can enact no law. The only effect, therefore, of his withhold-ing his approval of a bill passed by Congress is to suffer the existing laws to remain unchanged, and the delay occasioned is only that required to enable the States and the people to consider and act upon the subject in the election of public agents who will carry out their wishes and instructions. Any attempt to coerce the President to yield his sanction to measures which he can not approve would be a violation of the spirit of the Constitution, palpable and flagrant, and if successful would break down the independence of the executive department and make the President, elected by the people and clothed by the Constitution with power to defend their rights, the mere instrument of a majority of Congress. A surrender on his part of the powers with which the Constitution has invested his office would effect a practical alteration of that instrument without resorting to the prescribed process of amendment.

With the motives or considerations which may induce Congress to pass any bill the President can have nothing to do. He must presume them to be as pure as his own, and look only to the practical effect of their measures when compared with the Constitution or the public good.

But it has been urged by those who object to the exercise of this undoubted constitutional power that it asssails the representative principle and the capacity of the people to govern themselves; that there is greater safety in a numerous representative body than in the single Executive created by the Constitution, and that the Executive veto is a "one-man power," despotic in its character. To expose the fallacy of this objection it is only necessary to consider the frame and true character of our system. Ours is not a consolidated empire, but a confederated union. The States before the adoption of the Constitution were coordinate, coequal, and separate independent sovereignties, and by its adoption they did not lose that character. They clothed the Federal Government with certain powers and reserved all others, including their own sovereignty, to themselves. They guarded their own rights as States and the rights of the people by the very limitations which they incorporated into the Federal Constitution, whereby the different departments of the General Government were checks upon each other. That the majority should govern is a general principle controverted by none, but they must govern according to the Constitution, and not according to an undefined and unrestrained discretion, whereby they may oppress the minority.

The people of the United States are not blind to the fact that they may be temporarily misled, and that their representatives, legislative and executive, may be mistaken or influenced in their action by improper motives. They have therefore interposed between themselves and the laws which may be passed by their public agents various representations, such as assemblies, senates, and governors in their several States, a House of Representatives, a Senate, and a President of the United States. The people can by their own direct agency make no law, nor can the House of Representatives, immediately elected by them, nor can the Senate, nor can both together without the concurrence of the President or a vote of two-thirds of both Houses.

. . . The true theory of our system is not to govern by the acts or decrees of any one set of representatives. The Constitution interposes checks upon all branches of the Government, in order to give time for error to be corrected and delusion to pass away; but if the people settle down into a firm conviction different from that of their representatives they give effect to their opinions by changing their public servants. The checks which the people imposed on their public servants in the adoption of the Constitution are the best evidence of their capacity for self-government. They know that the men whom they elect to public stations are of like infirmities and passions with themselves, and not to be trusted without being restricted by coordinate authorities and constitutional limitations. Who that has witnessed the legislation of Congress for the last thirty years will say that he knows of no instance in which measures not demanded by the public good have been carried? Who will deny that in the State governments, by combinations of individuals and sections, in derogation of the general interest, banks have been chartered, systems of internal improvements adopted, and debts entailed upon the people repressing their growth and impairing their energies for years to come?

After so much experience it can not be said that absolute unchecked power is safe in the hands of any one set of representatives, or that the capacity of the people for self-government, which is admitted in its broadest extent, is a conclusive argument to prove the prudence, wisdom, and integrity of their representatives.

. . . In the exercise of the power of the veto the President is responsible not only to an enlightened public opinion, but to the people of the whole Union, who elected him, as the representatives in the legislative branches who differ with him in opinion are responsible to the people of particular States or districts, who compose their respective constituencies. To deny to the President the exercise of this power would be to repeal that provision of the Constitution which confers it upon him. To charge that its exercise unduly controls the legislative will is to complain of the Constitution itself.

. . . One great object of the Constitution in conferring upon the President a qualified negative upon the legislation of Congress was to protect minorities from injustice and oppression by majorities. The equality of their representation in the Senate and the veto power of the President are the constitutional guaranties which the smaller States have that their rights will be respected. Without these guaranties all their interests would be at the mercy of majorities in Congress representing the larger States. To the smaller and weaker States, therefore, the preservation of this power and its exercise upon proper occasions demanding it is of vital importance. They ratified the Constitution and entered into the Union, securing to themselves an equal representation with the larger States in the Senate; and they agreed to be bound by all laws passed by Congress upon the express condition, and none other, that they should be approved by the President or passed, his objections to the contrary notwithstanding, by a vote of two-thirds of both Houses. Upon this condition they have a right to insist as a part of the compact to which they gave their assent.

A bill might be passed by Congress against the will of the whole people of a particular State and against the votes of its Senators and all its Representatives. However prejudicial it might be to the interests of such State, it would be bound by it if the President shall approve it or it shall be passed by a vote of two-thirds of both Houses; but it has a right to demand that the President shall exercise his constitutional power and arrest it if his judgment is against it. If he surrender this power, or fail to exercise it in a case where he can not approve, it would make his formal approval a mere mockery, and would be itself a violation of the Constitution, and the dissenting State would become bound by a law which had not been passed according to the sanctions of the Constitution.

The objection to the exercise of the *veto* power is founded upon an idea respecting the popular will, which, if carried out, would annihilate State sovereignty and substitute for the present Federal Government a consolidation directed by a supposed numerical majority. A revolution of the Government would be silently effected and the States would be subjected to laws to which they have never given their constitutional consent.

The Supreme Court of the United States is invested with the power to declare, and has declared, acts of Congress passed with the concurrence of the Senate, the House of Representatives, and the approval of the President to be unconstitutional and void, and yet none, it is presumed, can be found who will be disposed to strip this highest judicial tribunal under the Constitution of this acknowledged power—a power necessary alike to its independence and the rights of individuals.

For the same reason that the Executive veto should, according to the doctrine maintained, be rendered nugatory, and be practically expunged from the Constitution, this power of the court should also be rendered nugatory and be expunged, because it restrains the legislative and Executive will, and because the exercise of such a power by the court may be regarded as being in conflict with the capacity of the people to govern themselves. Indeed, there is more reason for striking this power of the court from the Constitution than there is that of the qualified veto of the President, because the decision of the court is final, and can never be reversed even though both Houses of Congress and the President should be unanimous in opposition to it, whereas the veto of the President may be overruled by a vote of two-thirds of both Houses of Congress or by the people at the polls.

It is obvious that to preserve the system established by the Constitution each of the coordinate branches of the Government—the executive, legislative, and judicial—must be left in the exercise of its appropriate powers. If the executive or the judicial branch be deprived of powers conferred upon either as checks on the legislative, the preponderance of the latter will become disproportionate and absorbing and the others impotent for the accomplishment of the great objects for which they were established. Organized, as they are, by the Constitution, they work together harmoniously for the public good. If the Executive and the judiciary shall be deprived of the constitutional powers invested in them, and of their due proportions, the equilibrium of the system must be destroyed, and consolidation, with the most pernicious results, must ensue—a consolidation of unchecked, despotic power, exercised by majorities of the legislative branch.

The executive, legislative, and judicial each constitutes a separate coordinate department of the Goverment, and each is independent of the others. In the performance of their respective duties under the Constitution neither can in its legitimate action control the others. They each act upon their several responsibilities in their respective spheres. But if the doctrines now maintained be correct, the executive must become practically subordinate to the legislative, and the judiciary must become subordinate to both the legislative and the executive; and thus the whole power of the Government would be merged in a single department. Whenever, if ever, this shall occur, our glorious system of well-regulated self-government will crumble into ruins, to be succeeded, first by anarchy, and finally by monarchy or despotism. I am far from believing that this doctrine is the sentiment of the American people; and during the short period which remains in which it will be my duty to administer the executive department it will be my aim to maintain its independence and discharge its duties without infringing upon the powers or duties of either of the other departments of the Government.

The power of the Executive veto was exercised by the first and most illustrious of my predecessors and by four of his successors who preceded me in the administration of the Government, and it is believed in no instance prejudicially to the public interests. It has never been and there is but little danger that it ever can be abused. No President will ever desire unnecessarily to place his opinion in opposition to that of Congress. He must always exercise the power reluctantly, and only in cases where his convictions make it a matter of stern duty, which he can not escape. Indeed, there is more danger that the President, from the repugnance he must always feel to come in collision with Congress, may fail to exercise it in cases where the preservation of the Constitution from infraction, or the public good, may demand it than that he will ever exercise it unnecessarily or wantonly.

BIBLIOGRAPHICAL AIDS

The emphasis in this and subsequent volumes in the *Presidental Chronologies* series will be on the administrations of the presidents. The more important works on other aspects of their lives, either before or after their terms, are included since they may contribute to an understanding of the presidential careers.

The following bibliography is critically selected. An extensive biliography on Polk's entire life may be found in the Sellers' biography (See biographies below) and in the standard guides. The student might also wish to consult *Reader's Guide to Periodical Literature* and *Social Sciences and Humanities Index* (formerly *International Index*) for recent articles in scholarly journals.

Additional chronological information not included in this volume because it did not relate directly to the president may be found in the *Encyclopedia of American History,* edited by Richard B. Morris, revised edition (New York, 1965).

Asterisks after titles refer to books currently available in paperback editions.

SOURCE MATERIALS

The *Diary* of James K. Polk is the one best source for understanding the man and the President. Polk's *Diary* impresses the reader not only because of its readability, but also because of its insights into Polk's personality. It has an abundance of entertaining sidelights about some of the most influential nineteenth century Americans. Moralistic, gossipy, and informative, the *Diary* provides the reader with a certain kind of literary satisfaction. The Milo M. Quaiffe edition of *The Diary of James K. Polk During His Presidency,* four volumes, Chicago, 1910, is still the most essential source for the Presidential years. A more popular version, but too much an abridgement is *The Diary of a President 1845-1849,* Allen Nevins, editor, New York, 1929. It is good reading, but one wonders what was omitted. Polk's *Presidential Papers* are held and microfilmed by the Library of Congress, Washington, D.C. The entire collection is intact in forty-eight volumes and thirty-six boxes. The Nashville, Tennessee Historical Society holds an additional source of Polk's papers and correspondence, especially those dealing with his years of service to the state.

Polk-Bancroft Pape: ;, New York Public Library. George Bancroft's manuscript copies of many of Polk's papers. Four volumes of Polk's letters are included. Important and useful sources for an understanding of the complex foreign policy of the Polk years.

White, Robert H., ed. *Messages of the Governors of Tennessee.* 3 vols. Nashville, 1952--. Three volumes are complete. Tennessee's political history, excerpts from newspapers, and legislative history are included.

BIOGRAPHIES

McCormac, Eugene I. *James K. Polk, a Political Biography.* New York, 1922. McCormac places Polk within the context of a great statesman, and he notes the poor treatment accorded Polk by post-Civil War historians.

McCoy, Charles A. *Polk and the Presidency.* Austin, 1960. The author feels Polk belongs among America's great chief executives because of his dynamic use of Presidential powers, and his direction of the Mexican War.

Sellers, Charles G. *James K. Polk.* Vol. I: *Jacksonian, 1795-1843.* Princeton 1957. A masterful, scholarly portrayal of Polk's early career.

————.*James K. Polk.* Vol. II: *Continentalist,* 1843-1846. Princeton, 1966. Follows the course of political events in Polk's life, but ends before any real engagements in the Mexican War. The third and final volume of Sellers' biography has not yet been published.

ESSAYS

Overly brief descriptions of the Polk administration are contained in the *Encyclopedia Britannica,* and the *Americana Encyclopedia.* The research student should not rely on either of these for any substantial information. Eugene I. McCormac's treatment of Polk in the *Dictionary of American Biography* is a very good, but brief, sketch of Polk's career. The sources mentioned by McCormac are worth noting.

Abernathy, Thomas P. "The Origin of the Whig Party in Tennessee", *Mississippi Valley Historical Review,* March, 1926, 504-522. Traces the elements that led to some of the painful political experiences of James K. Polk as a state leader.

Graebner, Norman A. "James K Polk: a Study in Federal Patronage", *Mississippi Valley Historical Review,* June, 1952, 613-632. An elucidating account of the spoils system which plauged Polk's White House days.

Lavender, David. "How to Make it to the White House Without Really Trying", *American Heritage,* June 1967, 26. An amusing account of how General Zachary Taylor used James K. Polk to feather his own political nest.

Morris, Richard B. *Great Presidential Decisions.* New York, 1965*, 152-157. A highly provocative account of Polk's actions.

Sellers, Charles G. "Banking and Politics in Jackson's Tennessee", *Mississippi Valley Historical Review,* June, 1954, 61-84. Background for Polk's economic stand as a national leader.

MONOGRAPHS AND SPECIAL AREAS

Adams, Ephriam D. *British Interests and Activities in Texas, 1838-1846.* Baltimore, 1910. Details tensions between Texas and Mexico concerning possible United States annexation.

Bemis, Samuel F. *Latin-American Policy of the United States.* New York, 1943. A spirited defense of Polk's war policy.

Chase, Lucien B. *History of the Polk Administration.* New York, 1850. Chase defended the Polk administration, and served as a Democratic spokesman to retort Whig criticism.

DeVoto, Bernard. *1846, Year of Decision.* Boston, 1943. A very readable and exciting account of that famous year.

Henry, Robert S. *The Story of the Mexican War.* Indianapolis, 1950. Good military history of the war. Tends to minimize American reaction to Slidell's mission.

Hofstadter, Richard. *Anti-intellectualism in American Life.* New York, 1964. Chapter six, "The Decline of the Gentleman", traces the growth of democracy and its effects on the south and the west.

James, Marquis. *Andrew Jackson: Portrait of a President.* New York, 1937. Details relationship between Jackson and Polk. Well worth investigation for factual data, as well as literary pleasure.

Reeves, Jesse S. *Ameccan Diplomacy under Tyler and Polk.* Baltimore, 1907. One of the first studies of the importance of Polk's administration for the successful conclusions of the Oregon controversy and the Mexican War.

THE ERA OF EXPANSION

Andrist, Ralph K. ed. *The American Heritage History of the Making of the Nation.* New York, 1968, 257-282. A luxurious treatment of the Polk years, studded with illustrations.

Bailey, Thomas A. *A Diplomatic History of the American People.* New York, 1947. Chapters 14 and 15 considers the tumult of the period with humor and fact.

Bemis, Samuel F. *Diplomatic History.* New York, Fourth Edition, 1955.

Billington, Ray A. *Westward Expansion.* New York, 1949.

————. *The Far Western Frontier,* New York, 1956. Billington presents the colorful panorama of California and Oregon in a most satisfying manner.

Bills, A.H. *Rehearsal for Conflict.* New York, 1947.

Craven, Avery O. *The Growth of Southern Nationalism.* Baton Rouge, 1953. A fundamental study of many of the forces that made Polk what he was.

Henry, R.S. *The Story of the Mexican War.* New York, 1950.

Parkman, Francis. *The Oregon Trail.* New York, 1849. Still a classic.

Russell, R.R. *Economic Aspects of Southern Sectionalism, 1840-1861.* New York, 1924.

Smith, Justin H. *The War with Mexico.* 2 vols. New York, 1919. The author, using numerous sources, justifies the United States military action against Mexico.

Stephenson, N.W. *Texas and the Mexican War.* New York, 1921. A volume in the *Chronicles of American Series.* A brief but exciting history.

THE PRESIDENCY

American Heritage Publication. *History of the Presidents of the United States.* New York, 1968. A lavishly illustrated and informative discussion of the men in the White House.

Bailey, Thomas A. *Presidential Greatness: The Image and the Man from George Washington to the Present.* New York, 1966.* An entertaining and instructive volume. Bailey considers the qualities of presidential greatness, and James K. Polk is judged "little better than average." Bailey thinks Polk is "generally overrated," but still the strongest President between Jackson and Lincoln.

Binkley, Wilfred E. *The Man in the White House: His Powers and Duties.* Revised edition, New York, 1964.

Corwin, Edward S. *The President: Office and Powers.* Fourth edition, New York, 1957.

Kane, Joseph N. *Facts About the Presidents.* New York, 1959. A useful listing of data about each President, his cabinet, his personal life, and his achievements.

Laski, Harold J. *The American Presidency.* New York, 1940.

Morris, Richard B. *Great Presidential Decisions.* New York, 1961.* Morris focuses on the causes and effects of Polk's decisions related to the Mexican War.

Schlesinger, Arther M. "Historians Rate United States Presidents," *Life,* Nov. 1, 1948, 65. Polk ranked tenth in ranks of American Presidents rated on executive performance. Polk is thus judged to be "near great."

————. "Our Presidents: A Rating by Seventy-five Historians," *New York Times Magazine,* July 29, 1962, 12ff. In this poll, Polk advanced to eighth place, and tied with Harry Truman in the "near great" category.

NAME INDEX

Aberdeen, Lord, 15
Adams, Charles F., 20
Adams, John Q., 5
Allen, William, 8
Ampudia, General, 51

Baldwin, Robert, 11
Bancroft, George, 8, 10, 11, 12, 16
Bell, John, 4
Bibb, Mortimer, 10
Birney, James G., 9
Brady, Matthew C., 21
Buchanan, James, 6, 7, 10, 13, 14, 18, 53
Butler, William O., 18

Calhoun, John C., 5, 6, 7, 10, 21
Carson, Kit, 17
Cass, Lewis, 6, 7, 8, 18, 19
Clay, Henry, 3, 7, 9
Clifford, Nathan, 19
Crockett, David, 2

Dallas, George M., 8
Davis, Jefferson, 17
Dodge, Henry, 19

Fillmore, Millard, 19
Frelinghuysen, Theodore, 7
Frémont, John C., 15, 16, 20

Grier, Robert C., 15
Grundy, Felix, 1

Harrison, William H., 6
Herrera, Jose J., 13, 17

Jackson, Andrew, 2, 3, 4, 5, 7, 9, 11, 77
Johnson, Cave, 7, 10
Jones, James C., 6

Kearney, Stephen W., 14, 16

Lafayette, Marquis de, 2

Madison, Dolly, 21
Marcy, William, 10
Mason, John Y., 10, 16
McDowell, Ephraim, 1
McGuffey, William, 20
McLane, Louis, 13
Medary, Samuel, 8

Montgomery, John B., 15
Mott, Lucretia, 19

Nelson, John, 10

O'Sullivan, John L., 12

Pakenham, Richard, 12, 53
Paredes, Mariano, 13
Parrott, William S., 11
Pena y Pena, Manuel, 18
Picos, Andres, 16
Polk, Ezekiel, grandfather, 2
Polk, Frank, brother, 3
Polk, Jane Knox, mother, 1
Polk, John, brother, 3
Polk, Marshall, brother, 3
Polk, Samuel, father, 1, 3
Polk, Samuel, brother, 5
Polk, Sarah Childress, wife, 2, 5, 22

Revere, James W., 15

Santa Anna, Antonio, 16, 17, 58
Scott, Winfield S., 16, 17, 18
Slidell, John, 11, 12, 13, 14
Sloat, John D., 12, 15
Snively, Major, 44
Stanton, Elizabeth C., 19
Stewart, John, 7
Stockton, Robert F., 12, 15, 16
Story, Joseph, 15
Sully, Thomas, 17
Sutter, Johann A., 18

Taney, Roger B., 9
Taylor, Zachary, 11, 13, 16, 19, 20, 21, 49
Toucey, Isaac, 19
Trist, Nicholas P., 17, 18, 63, 73
Tyler, John, 6, 7, 9

Van Buren, Martin, 4, 5, 6, 7, 8, 19, 20

Walker, Robert J., 10
Wickliffe, Charles A., 10
Wilkins, William, 10
Wilmot, David, 15
Woodbury, Levi, 7, 11
Worth, William J., 16
Wright, Silas, 7, 8

92